# Secrets of Mesoamerica

## What Did the Aztec, Maya, and Olmec Really Know?

**Alda Dagny**

# Table of Contents

# Introduction

In modern times, we are surrounded by constant innovations and technological advancements in our societies. We are therefore often fascinated by how ancient civilizations were able to survive with much less than what we have available to us today.

Mesoamerican, Egyptian, Mesopotamian, and Chinese nations are all great examples of this. Researchers and archeologists are constantly looking for clues into their respective capabilities and achievements despite their lack of available resources.

When looking back, hundreds of questions race through our minds: Who were these civilizations? How did they survive? How did they come up with new ideas, considering the lack of communication and information available to them? Why do we still remember these civilizations? And more importantly, how did these civilizations shape the modern world?

We tend to believe that it would be nearly impossible to live without the commodities and the knowledge that we have today. However, what we fail to realize is that these civilizations not only survived, but they thrived!

The Mesoamerican native civilizations were among the first to live in the Americas, and they made a great impact in shaping Central America into what it is currently. Many influences that are present in South and Central American cultures today can be traced back to this time period.

The exact time has not been firmly established, however, archeologists estimate that the Mesoamerican civilizations dated as far back as 7,000 B.C.E. Even back then, they were fully functional and able to live comfortably up until the Spanish conquest in the 16th century, which saw the last of these empires.

What draws people to Mesoamerican history in particular is that they were oddly developed, organized, advanced, and structured for their time. This is a factor that surprised and amazed the European nations that discovered Mesoamerica. Some of their innovations even equaled or exceeded those of the "civilized" world. Through journal entries of explorers, we got to see firsthand accounts of how Europeans were in awe of what they found hidden in the jungles of the Americas. It was unlike anything that they had expected to find. Some had already explored other continents, such as Africa, and expected the New World to somewhat resemble the simplicity of the African savannah and population at the time. Instead, they came across complex mathematics, large and well-built structures, as well as people that were highly sensitive and knowledgeable about the universe.

The exact order of the Mesoamerican cultural development from the time of the first settlers can clearly be represented by the following order:

1.  Hunter/gatherer period

2.  Herding and agriculture

3.  Pottery revolution

4.  Social structures formation

5.  Surgical practices and scientific advancement

Without the technology and methods of communication that exist today, it is mind-blowing that these cultures were able to accomplish so much, and so efficiently. It is believed that the Olmec, specifically, made great headway in advancing their nation. The Maya and Aztec then piggybacked off of the Olmecs' work and advanced even further from there.

While there are certainly common factors among all the Mesoamerican groups, there are also distinct differences. The latter has aided historians and archeologists to identify each group and what made them unique, especially considering the lack of written information or witnesses to explain how these civilizations came about and lived.

Differences aside, civilizations in that area were able to coexist, and even interacted occasionally, such as on market days or for trading. However, this was a rarity for the ancient civilizations, as more often than not, they would tend to be very protective of their territories and were not welcoming to strangers. This trend would continue up until the Aztecs, who were known as a war society, and therefore were more prone to conducting battles with other tribes.

While we may have the preconceived idea that this was a time where development and lifestyle were very basic, it was also a time of great cultural and intellectual growth. Much of what was implemented and discovered in the Mesoamerican civilizations has carried through to modern times and has aided in advancing our current societies.

For instance, historians have found many similarities between the Mesoamerican civilizations, the Chinese beliefs, and the Egyptian structures. What perplexes archeologists to this day is that there was no communication between these nations. The Mesoamericans were totally isolated at the time, and yet we can trace striking similarities between them and other nations. Through this book, we will examine each Mesoamerican empire to determine whether these coincidences stem from a natural desire in human beings to achieve common goals, or whether there is more mystery behind what these civilizations knew.

# Location

The name "Meso" derives from the Greek word, which means "middle". This gives us a perfect indication of where Mesoamerica would be situated. Stretching from Mexico through to Honduras, the Mesoamerican cultures had a massive impact on the rest of the continent, and their reputation stretched globally. Although the occupied Mesoamerican territory spanned across Guatemala, Belize, and El Salvador, the civilians stayed predominantly in the Mexico area.

When looking at the grand scheme of the world map, the area might not appear to be large. However, there have been thousands of archeological sites found throughout Mesoamerica. Despite this, it is estimated that less than one percent of ruins have been worked on (*Archaeology and the Book of Mormon*, 2021). This is very significant, as it leads us to believe that there is still a large number of ruins to be uncovered, which could lead to an expanse of territory being discovered.

A great benefit for historians and archaeologists is that the cities and locations of the Mesoamerican civilizations were so widely spread out that they were able to gain insight into the lifestyle of each group by their location. Ranging from dense inland jungle areas to coastal and barren land, the Mesoamerican territory has vast natural habitats, and each empire had to adapt to the land that they had chosen to settle on. It is, therefore, interesting to observe how each state cultivated the land that they had, and how this impacted each group's ability to learn and develop while settling in those areas.

Another advantage of having states spread out across several countries was that extensive trade routes were created, which allowed commerce to play an important role in the lives of the local Mesoamerican civilizations.

# Groups

There are countless civilizations that occupied the Mesoamerican territory, however, three main groups of people garner the most attention.

The first and oldest group were the Olmecs, followed by the Maya, and then lastly, the Aztecs. It is hard to believe today, but prior to the Spanish conquest, there was no European-based language in Central and South America. Each group had their own dialect, and most of what we know today was named either by the European conquerors or by archeologists. In a nutshell, even the Olmecs, Mayans, and Aztecs called themselves by different names in their time!

There are said to be 14 Pre-Columbian forms of writing that are traced back to the Mesoamerican groups. The writing at the time was used mainly for names of civilians, as well as for notable places. However, archeologists are still working towards uncovering other scripts, which could provide further insight into their languages. Some of these languages worked their way through time, and to this day, some descendants of these civilizations are able to speak these native languages, such as the Nahua.

Each nation was vastly unique, having its own leaders and culture. They were seen as individual countries, so to speak, and were not all under one rulership or a common set of laws. This allowed each group to be unique and to develop in a way that separated them from the others. Their differences can be identified by the style of their art and ceramics, as well as in their inventions and belief systems.

When we think of the Mesoamerican cultures, some things that come to mind are gold, pyramids, statues, and perhaps even sacrifices or rituals. While these are all historically accurate, there is much more depth to these groups of people than what pops up in our initial thoughts.

These groups of individuals were required to eat, drink, raise children, and further develop their society and culture without any assistance from outside of their territories. It is safe to say that the Mesoamericans not only fulfilled these basic needs, but that they far exceeded them, and were able to create a reputable and awe-inspiring name for themselves. Although their nations were eventually brought to an end, the names Maya and Aztec are still easily recognizable today, despite the many hundreds of years that have passed since these empires were fully functioning.

Throughout this book, we will further explore what attributes made the three main Mesoamerican groups unique, and also consider how the civilization as a whole made great progress and advancement over time. In order to gain a good understanding, we will need to rely heavily on archeological findings, coupled together with a healthy imagination and ability to put ourselves in the midst of these civilizations!

# Chapter 1:

# Olmec Civilization

The Olmec civilization is known for being the innovators, and in a way, the "trend-setters" for the rest of the Mesoamerican civilizations. It is believed that the Olmecs were the first to develop a written language in the Americas, as well as the nation that discovered the rubber-making process. They had discovered the method by converting latex from the bark of the rubber tree and hardening it, in order to make rubber as we use it today. For their time, this was quite a feat! Although their name might not stand out as much as the other civilizations that would follow, such as the Aztecs, recognition must be given to the Olmecs for laying a foundation that would provide the rest of the nations with an opportunity to become great civilizations.

The Olmecs valued jade above all else and would travel far distances both north and south in search of the material. This created an impressive network for trading. Jade was used predominantly for ritual and worship purposes, as the blue color fascinated the Olmecs and led them to associate that stone with the rain and water gods who were prevalent in their society. The Olmecs were also avid art lovers. They quickly discovered that jade was an ideal material to use for their sculptures, as it left a smooth finish, and the coloring was unlike any other natural material that they would have had access to at the time in their region. Jade sculptures would later be discovered in Olmec territory, which would help historians understand who this nation was and when they were active throughout Mesoamerica.

Together with sculpting, the Olmecs also quickly partook in ceramics and pottery. Findings have led historians to believe that this skill was not necessarily discovered by the Mesoamericans themselves, but rather, that they were taught by other civilizations that were located further south. More specifically, the appearance of advanced-level ceramics happened quite suddenly, and there was no evidence of the Olmecs developing the art through trial and error.

The Olmecs were mysteriously destroyed, and while their end was rather abrupt, it provided the platform for the other civilizations to rise up and progress from the foundation that the Olmec had laid.

The Olmecs are considered the founders of the ancient Mesoamerican civilizations, however, they receive the least attention. This could be largely due to the lack of information that historians have on them, as well as their discovery being rather late compared to other civilizations, such as the Aztecs. Despite the great headway that they gave the other empires, their reputation, name, and achievements were largely eclipsed by the later Pre-Columbian civilizations. Further to this, the Olmecs had begun to develop a writing system, but were never able to fully implement this to the extent of documenting their history. Archeologists have therefore had to rely on their own interpretation, but much of the information that is in their possession remains a mystery.

## Geographical Location

The Olmecs had several sites where they operated from, however, the two most predominant cities were San Lorenzo and La Venta. The Tres Zapotes has become one of the most infamous archeological sites for excavations and history about the Olmec civilization. This can be found along the Mexican coast which, at the time, was a rather dry and barren land. However, scientists suspect that due to global warming, a large amount of water came into the region, which then became very tropical and lush. This would provide the perfect ground for planting and farming.

Many artifacts and belongings of the Olmecs were found scattered across the Mesoamerican region, which shows that they had an extensive trade route and that their merchants moved around a lot.

The Olmecs learned to create mounds and to build their homes on top of them, as this helped to keep the structures safe during floods. They purposefully chose areas that would face flash flooding, as this is what ensured great crops and successful growth of vegetation in the area.

As they were also settled along the coast of Mexico, they had a great dependence on the ocean. They would use the water to grow vegetation and produce, and they would also consume sea creatures, such as turtles and clams. Historians have been able to identify the contact that they had with the sea through their art, as some Olmec sculptures have featured various forms of saltwater fish, as well as some sharks.

# Background

The Olmecs were first discovered during excavations, where many large stone heads were found in the Mexican region. These portrait sculptures would become the defining trait of the Olmec civilization. It was initially believed that this was a nation that existed in a similar time period as the Mayans and they were largely pushed aside. However, a determined ethnologist, Matthew Stirling, and his wife were convinced that the Olmec were a far older civilization. Their theory was eventually proven to be correct despite the backlash that they faced initially. The Olmec had been around from about 1,200 B.C.E up until 400 B.C.E. This discovery stunned the majority of archeologists, as well as much of the academic world, as it showed how far back the Mesoamerican civilizations really went.

There is no discernible written work or language from the Olmecs, thus leaving much of their history and culture to the imagination. Archeologists have not found traces of a distinct language that was spoken by the Olmecs. In fact, they did not even call themselves the Olmecs, and no one is sure what their name would have actually been. The word "Olmec" was given as an after fact by the Aztecs, and comes from the word "Olmen", which means "Rubber People" in the Nahuatl language. This is a great pity, as the Olmecs have close to 2,000 years of history and culture, but most of it is undocumented. The Olmecs would write on paper, which was made from bark, but this paper was unfortunately not durable and would rot over time from humidity.

There is still a lot of information missing from this civilization, however, they did record their religious beliefs and practices. In fact, in the late 20th century, a stone slab containing engraved symbols was discovered. This slab was traced back to about 900 B.C.E. As the Olmecs were the first civilization to implement an organized religion, the civilizations that followed would adopt a similar method of worship.

Apart from religions, the civilizations that followed would also take on their calendar system, urbanization, ball games, and Pantheon-styled buildings.

At the onset, the Olmecs lived off of a primarily pescatarian diet, with occasional hunted meat as well. Over the years, the Olmecs settled close to rivers, as this was more productive for their regular fishing activities. They soon discovered that the riverbeds could provide good irrigation systems and would be great locations for agriculture. This was, in essence, the birth of farming in the Mesoamerican region. Once the crops began to grow, the Olmecs were able to include more variety into their diets, including maize, beans, and chilies. Their fishing villages would grow to farming villages, and soon afterwards, these would become intricate cities and urbanized villages.

Due to the abundance of food, the Olmecs did not require so many farmers to work the land. This opened the door for civilians to learn pottery and sculpting, as well as to build great structures for the city.

The city center was generally reserved for the upper class who dominated urban life, while the lower class would often live in small villages just outside of the city.

# Traits

While each civilization would have common denominators that were molded by the Mesoamerican territory, as well as by the influence of other nations, there were certain traits that were unique to each empire. These are the clues that historians look for when determining which nation they are studying, in order to identify each empire's unique achievements and insights.

## Building

The Olmecs are known for having quickly urbanized their land. The architectural layout and skill of many of the buildings, such as the religious centers, greatly impressed archeologists upon discovery of the Olmec territory. Their columns were often over 6.5 ft tall and made with precision out of basalt.

The trademark Olmec colossal basalt heads are studied extensively, and still marvel historians and archeologists. These heads would reach close to 10 ft tall and would weigh about eight tons! In total, 17 of these large sculptures have been discovered.

It is believed that the reason why the Olmecs focused mainly on sculpting faces instead of entire bodies was that they believed that the soul was contained in the head. The faces were generally flat with full lips. They would often be wearing helmets, or some sort of headgear. It is still largely unclear who the faces represent, however, many archaeologists believe that these could be tributes to leaders who had passed away. To this day, many historians still debate the origins of the Olmec population based on these sculptures. To some, the facial features largely resemble those of African natives, however, this would then lead to the question of how this African nation ended up in the middle of the Americas. To others, however, they believe that the features could stem from a population of ancient Asians who migrated to the Americas during the Ice Age period.

The Olmecs also did various paintings in rock caves, and made other forms of sculpture from jade, ceramic, and wood.

Oddly, their sculptures were mainly buried as a means to appease the gods. This was a great way for them to be preserved and helped historians to do extensive research after discovery.

As the Olmecs were one of the first Mesoamerican civilizations, many of the religious beliefs that would follow in other kingdoms originated from their practices. They believed in over eight different deities and were very loyal to their gods.

The Olmecs were also the first to construct a pyramid in the Americas, which stands at 112 ft tall, and was the largest structure of its time.

These achievements are very impressive considering there were no professional draftsmen. Moreover, the technology required to build such a lasting monument with accuracy and precision was severely limited.

Archeologists also found jewelry and jade masks that were made so precisely that they could have been manufactured with modern day technology.

The Olmecs have also been credited for being the first civilization in the Mesoamerican region to come up with aqueducts.

What has impressed archeologists the most was their premeditated architectural structures, as we can clearly see that the cities were well thought out, and construction was not done at random.

In some cities, there is a clear symmetry along the north axis and the south axis, and usually four colossal heads were placed to point outwards at key points. It is said that the number "four" was used to represent all of the axes, serving as a means of spiritually protecting the entire city from all directions.

## Spiritual

As with most things, the Olmecs had laid the foundation of religion for the rest of the civilizations that followed to build upon. They had a great reverence for animals, specifically those that they were in direct contact with, and many of their gods were depicted as one of these animals, a combination of two animals, or even a combination of animal and man. The sky dragon and were-jaguar were very common depictions amongst the Olmecs. They also believed that four dwarf-like people held up the sky, one for each axis. Unlike the later civilizations who liked their gods and sculptures to be represented by intimidating and large warriors, the Olmecs even had a baby rain god, who was depicted as a toothless infant.

They were also drawn to locations where natural elements were prominent and could be connected to other symbolic concepts. For instance, caves were a great place for rituals and worship, as they could lead to water, but also represented the underworld.

Certain representations of their gods were later found in Aztec and Mayan art as well, and with each age, the sculptures varied or developed slightly from the previous empire. This is one of the main areas in which historians were able to clearly see an influence from the Olmec civilization on the empires that would follow. The basis for the Mayan and Aztec religions and belief systems stemmed largely from the Olmecs.

# Fall of the Empire

The end of the Olmec empire remains largely mysterious and many details are still unknown. Historians and archeologists suspect that the population was driven out of their villages due to severe natural circumstances, such as a shortage of water supply, or an increase of volcanic activity.

Some theories have emerged that the Olmec deliberately destroyed their cities and monuments and moved along to somewhere else. Based on the strong evidence that the fall of the civilization was quite abrupt and no trace was found of them again, there is speculation that perhaps the Olmecs did not necessarily want to be tracked. After all, these civilizations did come from elsewhere on the globe, so it could be that migrating and ever-seeking new territory was simply part of their nature.

Another observation was that, in the later years, the Olmecs seemed to be reusing materials for their sculpting work. This has led some historians to wonder whether this meant that their trade roots had been blocked, either due to natural occurrences or because of hostility in the area. It would then explain the decline of the population, as they most likely did not have enough new produce coming in to sustain their needs.

For many years, historians believed that the civilization ended all at once and that there was some form of wipeout. However, recent evidence shows that the decline may have been more gradual, with each city taking its turn to fall.

An alternative theory is that the Olmecs didn't disappear, but rather, assimilated and joined other civilizations. Due to there being no clear reason as to why the empire disappeared so suddenly, some historians believe that when other empires started to rise up, the Olmecs decided to join their ranks in order to create a greater empire, in lieu of falling behind.

Unfortunately, unless there is a breakthrough in the archeological work done in Olmec territory, the answer may remain a mystery.

# Chapter 2:

# Mayan Civilization

If you have heard anything about the Mesoamerican civilizations, you have most likely come across the name "Maya". As one of the greatest groups of people in the ancient world, the Maya left a historical mark that has remained in modern times.

The Mayans ultimately emerged when the Olmec empire started collapsing. While they certainly learned and advanced a lot in their own right, they also copied much of what the great civilizations before them had done successfully. This influence can be seen in their social structures, religious beliefs, government, and urban lifestyle. The Mayans were very social, constantly building large gathering areas and temples, which encouraged the population to get together and socialize. They even invented sports fields and engaged in group ball games for entertainment!

There are many similarities between Mayan and modern day lifestyles. For instance, Mayans each had their own homes in which they permanently resided. They also lived in different cities with unique governing methods, laws, and rules to be followed. They followed a social hierarchy system largely based on individual accomplishments and the jobs that they would perform, which is also strikingly similar to modernity.

In the 21st century, nearly five million people are still able to speak some form of dialect from their Mayan ancestors. These descendants of the Mayan civilization still carry out some practices from their ancestors, including ceramics and religious rituals. Considering that the earliest settlers can be traced back to approximately 1,800 B.C.E, it is definitely an accomplishment to still have traces of the Mayans in existence today!

There are a few notable things that the Mayans were renowned for, including their calendar system, architecture, and mathematics. While these are perhaps not topics that one would expect to come out of an ancient civilization, this is only the tip of the iceberg when it comes to the legacy of the Mayan civilization.

# Geographical Location

The Maya territory covered the Guatemala region, as well as some parts of Honduras and Belize.

Unlike their counterparts at the time, the Mayans were largely grouped together, although not necessarily in the same city, and there is not much evidence to prove that they separated or scattered extensively to other regions.

The Maya had a total of 40 cities overall. Each city contained a population of up to 50,000 people, with a minimum of 5,000 civilians. In total, this means there were close to two million Mayan people at the peak of their civilization! Their cities were not only inland-based, as many were established along the coast lines, or on riverbanks. This was a great asset to the Mayans, as it would allow great opportunities for commerce and trading via the water passages.

Even after one city would peak and collapse, another would rise up out of the ashes of the previous one. This pattern continued until the ultimate fall of the entire empire.

It is due to the structure of independent cities that archeologists were able to uncover much of what we know about the Mayans today. Each city holds its own information, and when piecing it all together, we are able to put together the bigger picture of the empire as a whole. Today, many of the Mayan ruins and sites are open to the public to tour and witness the greatness of what this nation achieved. It is one of the few civilizations where this is made possible due to the sheer number of prominent sites that they had ruled over.

# Background

Settlers had come to the Mayan region of Mesoamerica from the locations we know today as Alaska and Siberia. The reason for this migration was to find warmer climates, as well as more fertile and workable land for agriculture. As they originated from barren and cold lands, the settlers were happy to find the Central American territory, which had an abundance of plant life, sunny weather, as well as animals and fish that could be hunted. Little did they know that the Mayans would go on to build one the world's most advanced civilizations!

Some theories have emerged that other civilizations that were around at the time, such as the Olmecs, may have foreseen that their nations were collapsing, and therefore joined the Mayan population. This could explain the sudden disappearance of those nations, as well as the advantage that the Mayans had in learning from the population that had preceded them.

## *Agriculture*

Early findings show that the Mayans started in the same fashion as many other ancient civilizations: with the hunter/gatherer method. This is man's most primitive instinct, so it is not surprising that it was adopted in the early days of the inhabitants.

They eventually moved on to agriculture, which played a key role in their civilization. Their main crops consisted of corn. However, other crops were also grown, such as beans, squash, and cassava.

The Mayans actually placed such a great emphasis on corn that in their creation story, they believe that great gods created humans out of corn. The Mayans believed that divinity could be found in all things, and that included their success with agriculture, as well as the natural factors that enhance or hinder their crops.

In addition, the development of the Mayan calendar was created as a means to track the agricultural cycles, and proved to be a great advancement for the Maya. They were able to develop this by tracking the sun and the sky while documenting their findings. This led to one of the greatest inventions of the ancient civilization!

Their agricultural endeavors were so successful that, more often than not, they had a surplus of food, which then allowed for massive growth in the population. They were among the first to cultivate crops and domesticate animals, such as dogs and llamas. They had also found a way to develop an advanced irrigation system and purify water for drinking.

## Trading

If you look at the geographic terrain of the Mayans, they were mainly in a dense rainforest climate. However, they were able to make do with the land and survive. Fortunately, there were also natural resources available to them, such as:

- limestone

- volcanic rock

- salt

- jade

- sea shells

From these resources, they were able to develop useful skills, such as pottery, and begin building and construction at scale. Once their ceramics had developed, it allowed them to begin trading with groups from surrounding territories, such as the Olmecs. While trading was a beneficial tool for the development of the Mayan society, it quickly led to social divide as well.

The population slowly separated into social classes, and a hierarchy was created. At the top of the hierarchy were the kings, who were said to be direct descendants of the gods, and they were followed by the wealthier traders and merchants.

The hierarchy system then spread out across the Mayan territory, and even resulted in some villages becoming more popular and powerful than others due to the amount of valuable resources that they had. The Mayans took full advantage of this regional trade, refining methods and techniques from the Olmecs, who were the oldest and most advanced of all the Mesoamerican civilizations.

## *Conflict*

Unfortunately, with power comes warfare, and the Mayans came into a period of civil war, as each city would fight to become the most powerful village.

The city of Tikal was known as the greatest city of the Maya civilization and could be considered its capital in today's terms. Tikal had an estimated population of about 100,000 civilians, which made it an extremely powerful state! The city of Calakmul, however, wanted to gain that power, which led to a long war between the two cities. Tikal eventually lost, and Calakmul took over as the most powerful state. Both cities would face their demise and collapse around the 9th century.

Thereafter, the city of Chichen Itza grew in size and power due to its close proximity to the sea, which made it the perfect location for maritime trade. This became a great time for cultural and intellectual growth. Chichen Itza became the first great Mayan city to do away with the traditional hierarchy in favor of a more democratic approach towards governing.

# Traits

When visiting a Mayan site today, some of the defining traits that stand out are the grand pyramids, elaborate glyphs and symbols, as well as the structure and precision of their buildings and temples. It is easy to get lost in time when visiting Mayan ruins, as many of them have been well-preserved by the jungle, and archeologists are able to identify the key attributes of the Mayan kingdom through the various sites.

## Architecture

The Mayan civilization is known for having built majestic urban centers with buildings made out of stone. These include large pyramids, which served as temples or religious houses.

La Danta pyramid is the perfect example of the masonry work done by the Maya. This structure is the largest pyramid in the whole of Mesoamerica, standing at an impressive 236 ft. Considering how primitive their resources were at the time, this was an astonishing feat, and many are shocked at the workmanship that it must have required to build such a structure in this time.

## Writing

The Mayans also developed a keen interest in writing. They were able to make paper from the bark of trees and would carve out hieroglyphics. These books became known as "codices". Interestingly, the codices are the only known system of writing in Mesoamerica! Other hieroglyphs were written by using their ceramics and stone structures.

A large number of these codices were found during excavations, and most of them were deciphered, which gave archaeologists a good insight into what was going on in the Maya civilization. In fact, prior to the deciphering of the hieroglyphs, archeologists believed that the Mayans were extremely religious and peaceful researchers. Many historians were desperately seeking a nation that would embody the idea of peace to counteract the many civilizations who were at war with one another, and they thought that the Maya were the perfect fit. The story that unfolded, however, was the opposite to their theory, and instead showed a nation that was constantly at war and performing rituals, such as human sacrifices. Since the beginning of excavations in the 1830s, almost all that is known about the Maya history has derived from the information contained within these hieroglyphs. This source showed that there were often battles among themselves for control over the bigger cities and the region as a whole.

The deciphering of the codices and hieroglyphs was such a tedious and complex process that it took most of the 19th century, and about 90% has been deciphered to date (Canadian Museum of History, n.d.). There are still some parts that require interpretation.

Apart from their calendar system, the Maya were also quite advanced in mathematics and invented the concept of zero, which was a great scientific breakthrough. For leisure, they made sports courts, where they could play group games with balls made out of rubber. It is said that the loser of the game not only had to face the humiliation of a loss, but was also then a candidate for the next human sacrifice. We will dive into this topic a little bit later.

## Swimming

We tend to think that ancient civilizations were incapable of swimming, or that they had a hostile relationship with any body of water. There is an incorrect idea that swimming was a privilege that was taught and learned by the upper class and civilized nations, and that this was reserved only as a luxury.

That being said, archeological findings have shown that the Mesoamerican civilizations had a positive experience with water, and that they were, in fact, good swimmers by today's standards. Considering that they survived by fishing, as well as by foraging the ocean's floor, it would make sense that they were in the ocean a lot more than the average person would be today.

Murals and depictions of the Mayans have been found by archeologists, and through these representations, the Mayans illustrated their civilians in various swimming positions, some of which can be likened to those that are common today, like the breaststroke.

In addition, archeologists have also found many seashells and other elements from the sea that cannot be found by walking along the beach. Sea creatures, such as turtles and sharks, were found to be a subject in many Mesoamerican artworks, which shows that they were skilled swimmers and often went into deeper waters. This is especially prevalent with the Maya nations that were located in cities close to the sea, such as in the Yucatan peninsula. However, there is less evidence of this type of sea-based artwork in the inland cities.

In written accounts, conquistadors testified that the local civilizations were extremely good swimmers, and would often throw themselves into the water during battles in order to mimic crocodiles and other creatures. They were defined as being great swimmers who seemed just as comfortable in the water as they were on land.

Children were taught to swim from a young age, which would ensure that they were skilled and comfortable in the sea and rivers by the time they reached adulthood. The Mesoamericans were also aware of the benefits that water had on the body and its ability to help fight illness and disease, similar to what we know as hydrotherapy in today's terms.

This trait was not carried down to descendants of the ancient civilizations, however, and many today are not able to swim. This could largely be due to the fact that the Mayans settled inland following the ending of the empire, and thus, the opportunity or necessity for being in the water faded.

# Warfare

War was an ever-present activity for the Mayan civilizations. The Mayan kings were usually brave and ruthless war captains. In hieroglyphics, these kings are often depicted wearing belts made of trophy heads to symbolize their victories and the eventual sacrifices of prisoners of war.

"Nacom" was one of the most important figures in the war. He was, in essence, the head of military strategy for the empire. His main responsibilities were to gather and organize the armies. This position, as well as other captains of war statuses, were reserved only for the elite and upper class. Soldiers were ordinarily taken from the middle class and commoners of the city.

In terms of weaponry, the most common weapon used was called the "atlatl", and was a type of spear that had a trajectory of approximately 150 ft. Other weapons that were used, and were generally typical of the time, were bladed spears, clubs, and axes.

Due to the jungle terrain, the Mayans often fought out of formation. They would first make use of the spears to fight off the enemies from a distance, and thereafter, they would finish off the battle in hand-to-hand combat with clubs and axes.

# Fall of the Empire

Similar to the Olmecs, the ending of the Maya empire is a rather mysterious one. Archaeologists and historians alike do not have a firm answer as to what happened and why the empires were abandoned so suddenly. A few theories are that the cities collapsed due to warfare, volcanic eruption, overpopulation, overuse of the land, or possibly a drought. However, the migration out of the Mayan cities was a slow process. As they were scattered throughout the region, each city would rise as another would fall, and after a brief period of great success, that city would also fall.

As the Mayan power started to decline, the Aztecs—who were situated in the northern region—started becoming more influential.

The Mayan population left their cities rather abruptly during the 8th and 9th centuries. By the time the Spanish conquerors had arrived, the majority of the civilians were living in agricultural villages and the structures were buried. This left a rather eerie feeling when explorers saw these massive cities now overgrown with plants and living harmoniously with the jungle.

The Aztecs wanted to unite with the few remaining Mayan cities to overthrow the Spanish conquistadors, but the Mayans were not open to this, which led to each nation fighting on their own from 1527 to 1530. The Spanish received constant back up, and eventually the remaining Mayan cities were conquered, with the inhabitants sent to live in Spanish settlements. The Mayans considered jade to be far more valuable than gold. When the Spanish conquest happened, many of the Mayan gold artifacts were melted down and used by the Spanish to make coins.

The population by no means had died down, and today, there are still an estimated seven million descendants of the Mayans that reside in the modern Mesoamerican region.

The modern day Mayans are still very much agriculturally inclined. They tend to live in communities and most women still wear traditional clothing. A large part of the population converted to Catholicism following the Spanish conquest, but some still practice the same religious rituals as their ancestors.

# Chapter 3:

# Aztec Civilization

Another prominent group of the Mesoamerican civilization, which was unfortunately also the last, was the Aztec tribe. As they followed the Olmecs and Mayans, their civilization was largely built upon a combination of both cultures and their traditions.

Covering an impressive 52,000 square miles, the Aztec kingdom was one of sheer power and decadence! The Aztec prided themselves in having a city that was not only practical and well thought out, but also beautiful to look at and completely jaw-dropping. Their goal was to impress any visitors and to ignite a jealous rage in their counterparts. It is no wonder that this civilization is still one of the most talked about from Mesoamerican history!

Although the city of Tenochtitlan was the pride and joy of the Aztec empire, it would also prove to be their demise. When the Spanish conquistadors saw the Aztec land in the 16th century, they were pleasantly surprised by its grandeur and magnificence, which ultimately landed the Aztecs on the "wanted" list of the European invaders.

The Aztec civilization can be divided into two main time periods:

1. Early Aztec Era - spans from the beginning of the 12th century until early 14th century and includes the founding of various states.

2. Late Aztec Era - from approximately 1325 onwards and included the building of the capital city, Tenochtichlan.

The Aztecs were known as a war society and they took their battles very seriously. Their warriors were fierce, brave, and dedicated. In an unlikely combination, they were also both scientific and spiritual. While these traits don't ordinarily go hand-in-hand, this combination adequately summarizes the Aztec empire.

# Geographical Location

The Aztecs settled on a territory that is now known as Mexico City. In the 13th century, a hunter/gatherer tribe called the Azta migrated from a place in the north called Aztlan. The Azta were told by the gods that they would settle at a location where an eagle was eating a snake while perched on a cactus. Legend has it that this is exactly what the tribe saw while traveling through Mexico, and thus, the city of Tenochtitlan was born. This is also the reason why the same depiction is featured on the current Mexican flag.

Unlike some of the other tribes, such as the Mayans, the Aztecs remained in the one and only city of Tenochtitlan. While the city was set up into regions, they didn't venture far from one another, and the entire population could be accounted for there. For this reason, the city of Tenochtitlan became urbanized and extremely powerful.

Even today, this city is still the capital of Mexico, and the current layout has been built off of the foundation of the Aztecs' design.

# Background

## *Triple Alliance*

The Aztec tribe was essentially a combination of three tribes, namely, the Mexica, the Texcoco, and the Tlacopan. These three cities put their forces together and joined to create an unforgettable empire, which would be known as one of the largest in the world. The Triple Aztec Alliance would allow them to conquer many other little cities and gain power throughout the land. When they would win a battle, the spoils would be split among the three cities. The Mexica, who would later become the Aztecs, would soon emerge as the dominating nation of the alliance. Although they arrived and settled in the 13th century, civilization really took off and gained a new level of power during the 14th and 15th centuries. They had a large amount of influence as well as riches across the whole of Mesoamerica.

By the 16th century, the Aztecs ruled over 500 states, and governed five to six million people! The city of Tenochtitlan alone held more than 140,000 people at its peak, which made it the most densely populated city in Mesoamerican history.

## *Trade*

Trading was an essential part of the Aztecs' survival and success as an empire. While regional trade in the traditional sense was performed, they were also one of the first civilizations to host regional markets. This innovation was a great success, and the neighboring tribes saw this as a convenient way to quickly exchange goods, as well as to socialize, which was a pass time that the Aztecs thoroughly enjoyed. Market days could attract as many as 50,000 people, which proved to be a great asset to the Aztec economy.

Some of the goods that were traded or displayed on market days included:

- gold

- turquoise

- cotton

- maize

- pottery

- tobacco

- beans

- cocoa bean

- greenstone

It was common practice for food, art, and slaves to also be sold at regional markets. For its time period, the market was a huge success, and a visitor would be almost guaranteed to find something worth trading.

The merchants often lived in a separated area of the city, and they would have very demanding jobs, as the goods would need to be transported by hand or carried on their backs. This would prove to be a great physical challenge that was taxing on the body. During tense times with neighboring tribes, the merchants would also need to play the role of spy, messenger, and informant. It is said that some even went as far as to wear disguises in order to adequately obtain information from enemies.

### *Food*

The staple diet of the Aztec was corn (maize). They also grew tomatoes, beans, squash, avocado, and chilies. While they were predominantly vegetarian, the upper class did have access to meat and fish; however, these were not consumed on a regular basis. All other classes would forfeit their meat, but would occasionally eat bugs, such as grasshoppers and spiders, as a source of protein.

The diet of the Aztec was overall quite well-balanced, with a mix of healthy carbs and starches, which sustained them through all the physical work that they did.

## Traits

Much of what is known about the Aztecs today can be found in written accounts of the Spanish conquistadors and clergymen who traveled to Mexico during the fall of the empire. Due to their letters and journaling, we have firsthand accounts of what everyday life was like amongst the Aztecs, as well as elements of their lives and civilization that were surprising to the Europeans at that time. The development of writing and glyphs, as well as pictures and art, also played a crucial role in providing evidence about the nuances of the Aztec civilization prior to its downfall.

## *Agriculture*

Agriculture was a crucial part of the Aztec way of life, as it permitted economic growth through the trading of goods. The Aztecs also created an effective irrigation system called "Chinampas", which was a small, man-made garden created above the waterline. Together with their canals, this allowed their crops to be successful and grow in good times. Due to this, Tenochtitlan would be similar to Venice in the ancient world, as there were a vast number of waterways and canal systems which would be maneuvered through on rafts. Floating and fixed flower gardens were also displayed among the canals and chinampas, which created a breathtaking landscape.

## *Urbanization*

As with many of the great Mesoamerican civilizations, the Aztec also built grand buildings and structures which would require impressive masonry skill. These structures would often be dedicated to the gods, serving as temples for worshiping and rituals.

The Templo Mayor Pyramid was one of these great structures. Sitting at nine feet high, it had a double staircase design which led to two separate temples on the top. This structure was very advanced for the time, and was said to have even impressed Hernán Cortés. Although the pyramid was destroyed by the Spanish, with a cathedral replacing it, the ruins can still be seen in Mexico City today.

Secret chambers were also discovered under this pyramid. Archeologists found elaborate depictions of the cosmic system underlined the pyramid's structure, and it was ultimately built to reflect what they had studied in the skies.

Similar to their predecessors, the Aztecs held a strict social structure and hierarchy. They were extremely urbanized, and like the Mayans, their governing structure could be closely compared to those that are found in modern times. Each region was closely monitored and would have to pay a form of tax or tribute to the ruler. The regions would pay according to their production, and special tax collectors had the responsibility of making sure that each region paid up accordingly.

They also had marriages that were formalized by a civil office, and courts of justice to settle any disputes between couples, as well as other matters.

Apart from the social aspect, the Aztecs were advanced scientifically and had their own calendar system, which they adopted from the Mayans. Their calendar would include a 260 day ritual calendar used by the priests for religious purposes, as well as a 365 day solar calendar.

Another trait that was adopted, this time from the Olmecs, was their love for art. Aside from sculpting, the Aztecs often acquired art pieces which would then be buried or displayed. The subject matter of Mesoamerican art would include animals, plants, and gods.

Art could also be used as a form of propaganda, and would highlight their ruler and his power, or show the consequences of a nation that displeased one of the gods.

## Language

They also brought with them a language known as Nahuatl. This became the official language of the region, and many words from Nahuatl would eventually be incorporated into the Spanish language, such as the word "chocolate".

The Nahuatl language was ultimately a shared language between the Aztecs and the Toltecs, as well as a few other minor cities in the region.

A significant amount of literature from the 16th century that was written by the Aztecs in Nahuatl was found during excavations. As a result of this, as well as from the written records by the Spanish conquistadors, many historians and archaeologists have confirmed the Aztec empire is the most documented of all the Mesoamerican civilizations.

## Clothing

The average Aztec citizen was clothed with plain cotton items, which were made to be more practical than fashionable. The women usually wore loose fitting skirts and blouses, while the men would wear a covering or apron-like garment.

People of a higher social standing would have additional adornments, which would become more elaborate the higher your ranking in society.

Women were often hired to weave clothes with bright colors, which would be reserved for the elite, the priests, and the warriors. They would also have the option of sporting a headdress and jewels.

Slaves, and those of the lowest class, would often just wear a simple garment for the ladies, and a plain loin cloth for the men.

When the Spanish arrived in Mexico, the difference in their attire was evident, and each nation was surprised to witness the garments of their opposition. Although, by today's standards, the Aztecs' clothing was not extremely out of the ordinary, the Spanish found that they were poorly and immodestly dressed when compared to the Europeans, who were covered neck down and had many different layers of clothing.

# Warfare

The Aztecs were advanced in their military prowess. They would often start wars as a means to get prisoners for sacrifices and rituals. In addition, many other cities attempted to overthrow the Aztecs in order to take over as the greatest empire of the time. This led the Aztecs to invest a lot of time and effort into ensuring that their army and weaponry was adequate.

Apart from the usual spears, clubs, and axes, the Aztec also came up with a new weapon: the blow dart. The tips of the darts would be dipped into secretions from poisonous frogs and inserted into a hollow tube that would serve as a gun. This tube was about five to six ft long, and was easy to carry around and use to eliminate enemies, as well as for hunting.

In a similar fashion to the Mayans, the leader of the Aztec empire was first and foremost a militant. The leaders were in charge of ensuring that the nation was led to great victories, and this would also aid in growing the empire.

The Aztecs also had a sort of conscription in place, which required all adult males to take part in battles. This was a great asset to their army's strength and allowed them to have a significant amount of manpower.

The warriors usually wore padded cotton armor and carried wooden shields which were covered in animal hide. The more senior and revered warriors were further adorned with animal skins and feathers, such as jaguar hide and eagle feathers, to accentuate their seniority, as well as to add a level of fierceness to their costume.

In Spanish eyewitness accounts and journal entries, they described the Aztecs as being incredibly vocal and intimidating during battle. They would distort their faces, scream, and make big movements which, coupled together with their elaborate outfits, would often throw off the Europeans, who were a lot more orderly and quieter in their demeanors.

# Fall of the Empire

Hernán Cortés, a Spanish explorer from a humble background, would be the key factor in the downfall of not only the Aztec Empire, but the ancient Mesoamerican civilization as a whole.

In 1519, Cortés—who could not find a purpose in Spain—set out towards the coasts of Mexico. This expedition was called off by Velázquez, but Cortés was a determined and defiant man who had his eye on the prize. He directly disobeyed orders and set out with a fleet of 11 ships, over 500 soldiers, 100 sailors, and close to 20 horses. His goal was to overthrow the civilizations that lived in the Mesoamerican region.

When they arrived at Tabasco, Cortés immediately burned the ships that they had arrived on in case his men changed their minds and decided to head back to Spain. This act alone is a testament to Cortés' determined personality and willpower. As they could not leave, the conquistadors were able to spend a lot of time observing and getting to know the natives of the land.

Cortés was able to form powerful alliances quickly and in large quantities. He was able to get hundreds of thousands of locals on his side against the Aztecs, many of whom had great respect for him and would shower him with gifts. He was gifted 20 women, one of which would go on to bear him a son. At the time, there were already instabilities with neighboring cities, and this allowed Cortés to form alliances that would aid him in overthrowing the Aztecs. In fact, one of the members of the original Triple Aztec Alliance, the Texcoco, turned on their own and joined forces with Cortés.

Despite all of their progress and strong military power, the Aztecs had an Achilles heel, and they would see their demise in the form of Spanish conquistadors.

The Spanish had been in the area seeking gold. The king of the Aztecs at the time, Montezuma II, believed that Cortés was a light skinned god that was visiting the Aztecs in order to fulfill a prophecy. Due to this, in November 1519, the Aztecs warmly welcomed and hosted Cortés among them and showered him with gifts, which included items of pure gold. This only motivated the Spanish further, as they had now perceived with certainty that gold was prevalent in the area, and Cortés could see great potential in making Tenochtitlan a European city.

Due to the prophecy that the Aztecs had, they immediately understood that the conquistadors would bring the fall of their nation. Legend has it that there was even an omen that appeared to the Aztecs on the eve of the fall of the Aztec empire, and they knew that this was the end.

The Aztecs were far more in number, but due to the more powerful and modern weaponry of the Spanish, they were overthrown and hundreds of Aztecs were killed. During this time, Cortés had received news that Spanish fleets from Cuba were on their way to arrest him for the defiant act he had committed against Velázquez. This led him to flee and leave his second in charge, Alvarado, to oversee the battle during his absence. The latter did not hesitate to fight, and he took the liberty of beginning a massacre on the Aztec people, which continued when Cortés returned.

It is said that the human sacrifice practices of the Aztecs were looked down upon by the Spanish, so much so that they were merciless when it came time to take the lives of the natives, including Montezuma, their king.

Those that had survived did not fare much better, however, as a wave of European diseases, such as smallpox, took over the land. The natives didn't have any immunity against this, leading to a mass wipeout of the nation. By 1520, the smallpox disease alone had decreased the population in Tenochtitlan by nearly half.

On August 13th, 1521, the Aztecs were completely defeated. Overall, 240,000 Aztecs were killed from the conquest. In the first century of the conquest, 90% of the native population had died, either from disease or violence (Gunderman, 2019). The city of Tenochtitlan was then torn down and a new city, Mexico City, was built from its ashes. Mexico City lies on top of the cultures from the Aztecs civilizations. In fact, the cathedral currently sits directly above the place where important Aztec rituals were performed, and their rich history can still be traced beneath the ground.

While this was the ultimate goal that the Spanish monarchy had in order to take over the New World, and Cortés had successfully managed to overthrow the greatest Mesoamerican empire at the time, Cortés' reputation back home was suffering greatly. Velázquez was extremely displeased at the fact that Cortés had gone on without him to the New World, and he was ensuring that everyone in power knew about this. This led Cortés to write several letters to the king of Spain, King Charles V, in which he explained his success stories and gave several accounts of the work he was doing in Mexico. These letters, which have since become known as the "Cortés letters", have been a great help to historians and archeologists in gaining insight into the Aztec culture, as they contain live accounts of what Cortés and his men had witnessed.

Today, descendants of the Aztecs still roam the land of Mexico. Although they are no longer prevalent in the capital city, they live in small communities across the countryside. It is estimated that about one and a half million Mexicans are Aztec descendants and can still speak the Nahuatl language today.

# Chapter 4:

# Mesoamerican Society and Politics

## Social Structure

When considering the development of Mesoamerican social structures, there are three main periods, which are referred to as follows:

1. Early Formative period (1500 to 900 B.C.E) - pottery period

2. Middle Formative period (900 to 300 B.C.E) - urbanization period

3. Late Formative period (400 B.C.E to 250 C.E) - individualization period

By comparing these periods, we can distinctly see how each civilization developed and iterated from a basic shared structure to grow from the previous period and become unique.

The average citizen of a Mesoamerican civilization lived in highly communal groups. The nobles were the only people that were allowed to show their wealth and wear jewelry.

The commoners, however, were divided up into groups, and were under the leadership of a nobleman and a council of elders. There was a big divide between the classes, and often there was no way to transfer from one social class to another. In other words, the class that you were born into, or that your family belonged to, would be the class that you were in for the rest of your life. Women were scarcely found in any form of leadership role, and they were mainly required to work in markets as midwives, or to assist the priests. The top positions were ultimately reserved for men. This included warriors, for which only men were recruited.

The emperor had personal residence, as well as royal property. Any land that was conquered during battles was henceforth in the emperor's possession and was generally given to nobles. The nobles could then choose to either evacuate the previous residents from the land, or more commonly, to let the residents live and work there with the requirement to share part of their earnings with the new noble owners.

Commoners were not allowed to own land, so they usually lived and worked on the land owned by the nobles. The nobles would then profit from the work done on the land at their discretion. The lower class were generally required to pay up to 30% of their produce to the overseers of their territory (Mexicolore, n.d.).

Although there were many similarities in their social structure, there were also a couple of differences, especially as one civilization took over from another.

## Olmecs

The Olmecs, being the first civilization, were the first to put in place a strict hierarchy among the population, ordered as follows:

1. Local rulers

2. Nobles

3. Commoners

4. Serfs

5. Slaves

This was a relatively fixed structure, and very rarely did someone move between any one of the classes, particularly those that found themselves in the lower classes.

## Mayans and Aztecs

Due to the Mayans being spread out across several cities, they had a different political system in each society.

In the city of Chichen Itza, for example, there was a joint rulership in effect, which was called the "Mutepal". This meant that the royal family jointly governed the country along with either the priests or the head of war.

In both the Mayan and Aztec empires, the monarchs were the ultimate rulers over all of the states, as they came from royal dynasties. Their power and control was based on the resources that they held, such as obsidian. The king or ruler of the society could not be captured or sacrificed, as they believed that this would upset the gods and lead to the occurrence of a natural disaster. This made them extremely powerful, as they were untouchable in the eyes of the population.

The rest of the population were categorized into the following groups:

- The elites made up about 10% of the population and included members of the royal family, who were said to be direct descendants of the gods. This class could also include priests and the wealthier civilians.

- The middle class consisted of lower level priests, soldiers, as well as merchants.

- The commoners were the farmers and laborers.

Both the Mayans and the Aztecs believed that obedience to people in leadership roles was crucial to the overall harmony of the universe. They were mindful of their position in society, ensuring that all was as it should be in order to keep a good and bountiful flow of life.

A recent study on 24 Mesoamerican civilizations showed that the reason why these empires lasted as long as they did, and went on to build reputable societies, was due to their social structures and governing systems (ScienceDaily, 2023). Many other civilizations with no form of classing system, and who were at the mercy of one single dictatorship, collapsed fairly quickly and did not achieve much by comparison.

Furthermore, throughout all the civilizations, the Mesoamericans had a particularly good work ethic, and from an early age, they undertook their responsibilities with much dedication and pride. They were encouraged to perform well, and everyone had their place and role to fulfill in order for the society to do well.

# Taxes

Even way back in the ancient Mesoamerican civilizations, there was a taxing system in place. This was known as a tribute and would generally be given in the form of goods, services, or labor, as there was no official currency in existence at the time. Each region was monitored based on their production and would need to provide a tribute to the debt collectors in accordance with their gains.

This tribute system was the main source of income for the empire. The tributes were collected either every 80 days, 6 months, or yearly, depending on the person's position. Merchants and frequent travelers could give their tributes less frequently due to their extended periods of absence from the city.

During battles, after a territory had been successfully defeated and conquered, the civilians of that territory were required to pay regular tributes to the victorious nation. For a nation that was often in battles and had very good warriors, like the Aztecs, this was a great way to increase money in the city.

# Slaves

Being a slave in Mesoamerican society was typically a form of punishment for either a crime committed or for not paying tribute. During battles, prisoners of war were also taken to become slaves if they were not required to be sacrificed.

Slaves were permitted to marry and to have children. There were also a few ways for a slave to receive their freedom, as follows:

- purchase freedom

- trade/substitute another person in their place

- death of the slave owner

- marriage to the slave owner

Overall, the conditions were not as bad as what we normally associate with slavery. Owners of slaves had to ensure that their slaves had a house to live in and food to eat. It was not legal to resell a slave after purchase, and the families were required to be kept together. Fortunately, children of slaves were not automatically considered slaves themselves. Every individual had to be pronounced a slave in their own right, and thus, it was not passed down by birth.

Therefore, by comparison to other cultures, the Mesoamericans were largely humane in their approach towards slavery and the treatment of their slaves. A person wouldn't become a slave just because of a prejudice, but instead, it was largely an alternative for imprisonment. The slave would still have the same benefits as a civilian, such as remaining with their families and being taken care of; however, the main difference was that they wouldn't be able to earn on their own, and ultimately, all that they worked for would go to their owner.

# Marriage

The Mesoamerican civilizations believed in a union between a man and a woman. Typically, the men would marry between the ages of 20 and 22 years old, while the women would wed between 15 and 18 years old.

The marriages were generally arranged by the families of the couple, who would choose the best suitor that would benefit both families and form a strong alliance. Someone could only marry someone else from their social class. For example, a noble was not allowed to marry a commoner. The marriage ceremony would last approximately four days and consisted of feasting, rituals, and music. These were generally seen as great events and as a big deal among the civilian population.

Polygamy was accepted at the time, and the man was permitted to have relationships outside of the marriage with any unmarried woman, including concubines.

The married couple could choose to separate if the court of justice saw fit, provided that the wife had already given birth to at least one son. In the event of a separation, the sons would go live with the dad, while the daughters would stay with the mom. It was very common in the Mesoamerican civilizations for the fathers to be the main person responsible for the upbringing of male children, while it was the mother's responsibility to do the same for the daughters. This was the case whether the couple stayed together or not.

# Women

Research has shown that women had a slightly contradictory treatment in the Mesoamerican society (Mexicolore, n.d.). Although it could be closely compared to the history of women in the European world, there were also instances where equality was a more common concept. Firstly, the Mesoamericans recognized that life could not come forth without the contribution from both a male and female. For that reason, they did not necessarily view the women as being incapable, weak, or beneath the male.

However, they did distinguish roles between a male and a female. Men were expected to do laborious work, while women were to be in charge of housekeeping and cooking. The gender-based roles were taken very seriously, and newborns were often gifted with an item that would represent the role they would fulfill later on in life. Little girls were given a bundle of reeds for sweeping, while boys were given a tool for manual work.

Usually in these historical instances, where work was separated based on gender, childrearing would automatically fall on the women. This was not the case with the Mesoamericans, however, and the responsibility of who would raise the child would be dependent on its gender. Fathers were expected to raise male children, while girls would become the responsibility of their mothers.

Both men and women were entitled to owning land, properties, or inheriting from family that had passed on.

In their religion, the Mesoamerican deities were not only reserved for males, but there have been sculptures and depictions of powerful female goddesses as well.

When it came to governing and politics, women were permitted to take up a leadership role in the Maya civilization. However, the Aztecs did not adopt this same approach, and politics was reserved for males only.

# Children

The Mesoamerican civilization generally treated their children quite well, and saw the value in educating and raising them well for the future benefit of their kingdoms.

All children were therefore required to go to school, taking specialized classes which varied according to their social class and gender.

Children in the upper class attended classes to become priests or government officials. The lower class children trained as laborers and general workers.

This once again demonstrates how the social divide in these ancient civilizations was largely set in stone. Once your family had been placed into a certain social class, there was little that could be done for a child to move to a superior class.

Children were required to start schooling at the age of six, and all training was completed by the age of 13, at which time they could put into practice what they had learned. Mandatory schooling was not something that was common among other nations in those days, usually only being reserved for wealthy or elite children. The Mesoamericans were therefore one of the earliest civilizations to enforce compulsory lessons and essential schooling for minors regardless of their social class.

Those called to serve as warriors would begin their combat training at the young age of 15. When a boy had reached the age of 10, he would be given a short haircut with a long lock at the nape of the neck. Once the boy had captured his first prisoner during battle, the lock could be cut off. This practice was used as a means to motivate the boys into achieving this goal, and once they were successfully rid of the lock, bragging rights were the order of the day!

Mesoamerican children would face harsh punishments if they misbehaved or rebelled, both in school and at home. However, in terms of lawful punishment, children were only deemed accountable at the age of 10 years or older. Thus, before then, they would receive a more standard form of discipline for the time, such as inhaling chili smoke or mild corporal punishment.

Parents were allowed to take their child to court in some cases, such as severe disrespect from the child, wastefulness, as well as showing acts of cowardice. Some of these crimes, if deemed serious and threatening to the nation, could be punishable by death.

# Law

Each state was represented by a supreme leader/emperor, a supreme judge, as well as an administrator.

The emperor, however, often had little to no power and influence. They were simply in the role because they were believed to have been direct descendants of the gods. Any advice would generally come from a council of nobles and elders. This could be likened to some modern day monarchies.

The laws in the kingdom were based on a royal decree which was passed down from generation to generation. These laws were written down in pictographs and used by judges as required.

Different court systems were in place, depending on the type of case:

- Criminal court - to solve any crime or offense

- Civil court - separation, domestic abuse

- Commercial court - disputes over trades or markets

- Religious court - priests, rituals, and sacrifices

The accused party was permitted to defend themselves by personal representation only, as there were no lawyers or attorneys yet, and they could call on witnesses when required to strengthen their case.

Further to this, all trials were held publicly, and were often a great source of drama and entertainment for the rest of the population. Crimes were not taken lightly and offenders were severely punished. The most serious crimes were considered to be theft and adultery. In some cases, the guilty party could have their homes destroyed along with all of their belongings. Other common forms of punishment included imprisonment, slavery, death sentencing, various forms of torture, and often a shaven head, which served to make a public statement of one's status as an offender.

There was a prison distribution system that was dependent on the crime that was committed and the level of its severity. The ultimate penalty was death row, followed by a prison specifically for debtor's crimes, and finally a prison for minor crimes.

The prison's conditions were severe, and many lost their lives while in custody. This kept the population in order, ensuring that there was ongoing respect for the ruling powers.

If a prisoner was convicted, the families of the victims or defendant could allow the accused to become their slave instead of facing the death penalty.

In the event that theft was committed, the criminal had the chance to pay back the value of what was stolen, or else they would become a slave.

Adultery laws were generally in the man's favor. A married man was permitted to commit adultery with concubines and with unmarried women. If adultery was committed with a married lady, then the man was found guilty of the crime. A woman, however, could be accused of adultery whether the act was committed with a married or unmarried man.

Another law that would be considered out of balance was the crime of public drunkenness. This was an act that was forbidden and punishable for the younger generation, however, it was permitted and acceptable for elders to be drunk in public.

# Chapter 5:

# Medical Advancements

In Mesoamerican civilizations, medical and spiritual practices often went hand-in-hand. The tribes firmly believed that any ailment, sickness, or injury that befell them would be a hand of fate dealt by the gods.

Their first point of contact when contracting an illness would therefore be the high priest, who would work together with healers and herbalists to pray and perform rituals before applying the necessary physical treatment.

When the Spanish entered Mexican territory and battled against the native kingdoms, they were highly surprised by the medical abilities of the natives, especially the Aztecs, who were their main opponents. In fact, in journal entries found later on, the Spanish confirmed that the Aztecs were excellent surgeons, and the Europeans learned some techniques from them. Some native healers were even able to cure Spaniards who had suffered from long term illnesses which were deemed incurable in Europe.

As with much of the Mesoamerican knowledge, the Aztecs had accumulated a wealth of information and practices that had been tried and tested by the civilizations that had come before them. This gave them a big advantage, allowing them to flourish in their territory with the elements that were available to them.

The healers, also called Shamas, had to go through a harsh selection process. In order to qualify as a Shama, one not only had to have a deep understanding of the body, but also an acute connection to nature and plants. The healers were required to get permission from the plants before using them in their remedies or rituals. A broad knowledge about the different plants and their benefits was also equally required to be a Shama.

There were various methods of diagnosing a patient. Usually, the healers would have a set of stones that was used alongside prayer, requesting for the gods to communicate and show them what the issue was with the patient. Another method was to look at the reflection of the person in water and, once again with a lot of prayer, the gods would reveal what ailment the patient was suffering from through the water.

Based on codices found during excavations, the Mesoamerican nations (especially the Aztecs) seemed to have three predominant impacts to their overall health: birth, battle wounds, and diarrhea. Many historians were confused as to why they suffered frequently from diarrhea, as they ate well and had drinkable water. However, this was likely due to the anxiety from constantly being in battle or being next in line for sacrifice. The constant unsurety and uptightness that the warriors must have felt on a daily basis was sure to have some effect on the body. Otherwise, the Mesoamericans were fortunate in that they did not encounter any major diseases or illnesses in their region until the arrival of smallpox with the Spanish.

Modern day Nahuas still use many of these medical practices, along with some techniques from Europe and other nations that have been put into practice since then.

# Spirit

In Mesoamerican culture, we cannot talk about medicine without mentioning spirituality first. The Mesoamericans were incredibly spiritual and believed that all things in their world had some significance to the gods. It is therefore no surprise that the Mesoamericans believed that any sickness or injury was a sign of a displeased god and a consequence of a deserved punishment.

The Mesoamericans believed that the body was made up of three main soul chambers:

- "Tonalli", which is located in the head, is linked to belief and faith.

- "Teyolia", which is located in the heart, is linked to knowledge and memory.

- "Ihiyotl", which is located in the liver, is linked to the supernatural.

In order for a person to function as they should and be in good health, a balance between these three souls needed to be achieved and maintained. Aside from regular prayer, rituals, and sacrifices, the Mesoamericans often also wore amulets that were blessed by the priests as a means of protection.

The Mayans, for example, believed that healing of the soul should be emphasized and made the main priority rather than healing the physical body, which would automatically follow once the balance of the soul was restored.

"Ch'ulel" is the concept of energy that is found in the body, which has an effect on everyone and everything in the universe. This can be likened to the "Chi" concept from China, or the Buddhist concept of "Chakras". In essence, the energy that is found in a person can determine the state of their health if not attended to properly.

A healer's main focus in curing a patient would be to first redirect the energy in their body and realign their three souls in order to put things back in balance. The gods would also be individually called upon depending on the ailment. For instance, the rain god would be prayed to for sicknesses related to wet or cold symptoms, and the patient would even travel to rivers in order to give their offering. Assistance from the "Flayed" god would be required for any skin-related ailments like eczema and rashes.

The Mesoamericans further believed that nature would punish your health if you had a hand in hurting the environment. They were therefore very respectful of their surroundings and treated every living organism in a delicate way.

Vegetation was believed to be a gift from the rain god, Tlatloc. It was therefore crucial to ensure that this god was pleased before using any of the herbs to cure a patient. This thought process was applicable to all of the elements involved in the treatment process, including water, fire, and produce. Due to this, they often worshiped the rain god to ensure that there were enough rain showers for healthy crops, but not too much such that they would be flooded out, thereby destroying lives as a consequence. Water shrines could be found around the temples for this purpose, and are still a tradition in some Nahua cultures to this day.

Unlike the more traditional way of being bedridden when recovering, the Mesoamerican patients would often have a jam packed schedule of healer visits, ceremonies, and many complex rituals. Sacrifices were often performed to ask the gods for forgiveness, as well as to ward off any evil spirits of sickness. The ceremony would be followed by a festival, where dancing, feasting, and drinking would ensue. The treatment of a patient was not a matter of privacy between patient and doctor, but it was a public affair in which the whole community got involved.

## Herbs and Plants

The herbalists would experiment with many different plants and often tested their medicinal uses. The Mesoamericans truly had a herb or a plant for every ailment that existed in their time and region.

The healers had a three-step process for treating wounds:

1. The wound would be thoroughly washed with warm water and sterilized with urine.

2. A herbal concoction would be mixed and applied to the wound, with various plants being used depending on the type of wound.

3. The wound would be dressed with hot sap and salt.

The sap that was used for dressing wounds was from an agave plant with antibiotic properties.

The Spanish conquistadors were astonished at how the natives knew the medicinal properties of every single plant and herb. Considering the hundreds of distinct flora in that region, it was quite impressive to their European counterparts.

The Aztecs even had their own botanical gardens in the city of Tenochtitlan. Some plants or flowers were specifically sourced throughout the region and were brought to the gardens for display and observation. Patients were given a combination of plants according to their ailment, with the stipulation that they would report back to the herbalists regarding the effects of the plant. This helped the healers and herbalists to build up a great repertoire on the medicinal values of each plant species.

The herbal remedies were often categorized into two main classifications: hot and cold.

The cold ailments—physical pain and cramps—were prescribed hot herbal remedies. The opposite is applicable whereby the hot ailments—fevers and food poisoning—were prescribed cold herbal remedies.

Plants, herbs, and flowers were also classified by color, and each color had its own significance in the treatment process as follows:

- red - blood-related issues

- blue - sedatives

- yellow - liver and spleen

White plants and flowers were avoided, as this color was linked with death in the Mesoamerican belief system.

Aside from coloring, plants and flowers with a sweet fragrance were considered to be rich in medicinal properties, while plants that lacked smell or taste were seen as having no beneficial properties.

The healers also made use of hallucinogenic plants, such as morning glory, as well as tobacco and alcohol to numb the pain and aid the patient in their recovery.

Another popular flower that was frequently used by the Aztecs was the Passion Flower, which is said to have properties that aid with pain and muscle spasms. This would have been a great help to patients in Mesoamerican times during births, surgeries, and as a muscle relaxant, considering the amount of physical labor that these nations endured. The flower is still used today as a herbal treatment and has been found to have additional benefits, such as lowering blood pressure and treating insomnia.

# Prevention

Due to the tropical climate, as well as the original food groups, the Mesoamericans were in good health overall. At the time, many of their European counterparts had diets that consisted of a lot of starch from wheat and potatoes, as well as butters, sugars, and oils, which were not healthy when consumed in excess. Therefore, their health was not as good by comparison, which led to frequent sickness and heart failure. Coupled together with the development of the wheel, the Europeans were not always as physically active or healthy as the Mesoamericans were.

The Mesoamericans also had access to foods that are highly recommended by dieticians, even by today's standards. These foods include chia seeds, avocados, fish, corn, pure cocoa beans (not mixed with sugar), and grains.

The chia seed, for example, comes from the Nahuatl word "chian", which means oily. It contains high levels of Omega 3 oil, which is good for the heart. This seed is still highly recommended by dieticians today, making it highly sought after.

Perhaps surprisingly, the Mesoamericans were also very hygiene conscious. Unlike other nations at the time, including the Europeans, the Mesoamericans bathed regularly and saw to their cleanliness as part of their daily routines. Apart from bathing for hygiene, they also believed that baths could cool the heart. In fact, the Mesoamericans bathed so often that the Spanish placed a ban on bathing in 1567 due to the frequent nudity and sexual connotation.

Excavations showed that the Aztecs even had a sauna-type structure, which consisted of a small room that was heated by fire from the outside walls. The Aztecs would throw water against the walls from within the room, which would create an abundance of steam.

These steam baths or sauna sessions, called "Temazcal", were used to treat coughs, fevers, joint aches, and skin diseases. Mint and sage herbs were used in the "Temazcals" in order to maximize the health benefits. This also mirrors many practices and resources that are used in modern times, such as saunas, humidifiers, and essential oils, in order to maximize health benefits.

The Mesoamericans also had good oral hygiene. This was also not the case for the Europeans at the time, as they were not aware of the consequences to the body if the teeth were in bad condition. The Mesoamericans, on the other hand, would clean their teeth regularly with charcoal and salt.

Using charcoal for cleaning teeth is also a common practice that is recommended in modern times, with many teeth cleaning products today containing charcoal and salt content. The Mesoamericans were ahead of their time with this discovery and saw the value of good dental care on the overall health of the body. When required, they were even able to insert dental fillings with fool's gold, or insert dental prosthesis using jade or turquoise stones.

At the time, the Spanish were rarely bathing, they were lacking vitamins, there was no real dental care, and they often had waves of contagious diseases that would wipe out the population. By contrast, based on these elements that were all incorporated into their daily routines, it is evident that the Mesoamericans were good at maintaining a good health condition overall for their time. This was a good way to prevent diseases and would ensure a quick recovery when they did fall victim to illnesses.

# Birth

The Mesoamericans placed great importance on the raising and nurturing of children, and they took this very seriously from the time of pregnancy. Rituals were performed on soon-to-be mothers before their babies were even born.

Professional midwives were trained and used for birthing. Similar to other healers, midwives were required to have a good understanding of herbal remedies, the body, and above all, the spiritual realm and its impact on the birthing process.

Aside from its other uses, saunas were also used as birthing centers, as the steam was believed to be a cleanser of the sexual sin from the parents which burdened the baby. Leaf fans were used to direct the flow of the steam towards the mother during her labor.

Tools and remedies were used simultaneously to aid the mother during labor and childbirth, including rattles and figurines of gods, which would ensure that the gods were appeased and present during the process.

If the birth was not progressing, the first step would be to perform blood-letting. Both the husband and the expecting mother were required to offer blood as a plea to the gods to save the baby's life.

In the event of the baby's death during labor, the parents were given two options:

- The baby could be removed to be buried under the house of the parents.

- The delivery room could be closed up, leaving the mother to succumb to death.

The latter was the more honorable option, as the Mesoamericans believed that the mother would then become a goddess. Not being able to deliver a baby was not seen as a failure on the part of the mother or the midwife, but rather, it was an honor for the mother to be chosen to join the gods on the sun, and for the remaining family to have a soul near the sun as their connection to the spiritual.

Tobacco and plants with numbing and hallucinogenic effects were administered in order to manage the pain, and stone knives were used to either cut the umbilical cord in the case of a successful birth, or to remove the child where birth was not progressing.

# Surgery

When bones were broken during battle, the Aztecs were able to successfully treat these injuries. Eyewitnesses have even recounted that not only could the Aztecs heal such injuries, but they could do so even faster than their European opponents.

"Trepanation" is the process of drilling a hole through the skull in order to relieve pressure. Evidence of this operation being performed has been found in Mesoamerica. This procedure requires extreme delicateness and precision, and is a very risk intensive surgery, even in modern times.

The Mesoamericans had an abundance of obsidian, which is considered one of the sharpest natural materials in the world, as it comes from volcanic glass. Obsidian allowed the healers to be extremely precise during their procedures, as it is even thinner and sharper than most modern surgical steel.

Various other surgeries were performed, such as the removal of tumors and the draining of wounds, as well as circumcisions for priests. Even by today's standards, these types of surgeries are extremely delicate, requiring highly skilled and reputable surgeons to perform them. It is therefore quite awe-inspiring to realize that these civilizations were performing these kinds of operations successfully!

# Chapter 6:

# Inventions and Progress

Perhaps the most astonishing fact about Mesoamerican inventions was not that such ancient civilizations were able to create these elements, but that they were also deemed "native", "wild", and "uncivilized" by other countries at the same time.

The Spanish were completely taken aback to arrive at an untouched land with native inhabitants and find signs of complex mathematical systems, writings, rubber, and large buildings. This was not what they had expected to find! Although they were fascinated, it also terrified them to know what the Mesoamericans were capable of, and they therefore believed that many of these creations were pagan works of evil spirits, which led them to largely destroy and abandon the inventions.

Today, we are compelled to discover all that the Mesoamericans achieved, and many expeditions have centered around finding out more about these civilizations. Research in these areas is still very much active, as there is much to be uncovered and many hieroglyphs that still require deciphering!

Many were surprised that the Mesoamericans did not invent the wheel, as miniature forms of wheels were found on children's toys. It is therefore questionable as to why they did not amplify the measurements and use a bigger version to their benefit.

Much of history as it had been known prior to the discovery of the Mesoamerican civilizations had to be re-examined, as credit had to be given to the Olmecs, Mayans, and Aztecs for being the first inventors as opposed to their European counterparts, who had originally claimed the title for themselves.

The South American civilizations had extremely difficult natural conditions compared to other civilizations at the time. In addition, other nations, such as Egypt and Mesopotamia, were in communication with one another, and would often exchange ideas or inform each other of new inventions and discoveries. On the other hand, the Mesoamericans were completely isolated, and any inventions that came about were purely from within their own ranks.

# Writing

Writing in Mesoamerica had been invented independently from the other cultures of the old world. This is also indicative of a common pattern that emerges across human civilizations as they develop. Namely, human beings tend to be drawn to finding methods of communicating, as well as documenting their perceptions of history. The Mesoamericans were no exception to this developmental milestone in human history.

The first form of a writing system in the Mesoamerican region was created by the Olmecs. This system was predominantly in the form of pictures or other visual representations, and had not developed to the stage of being an official language or script.

Historians are still seeking to determine whether the Mayans used what had already been created by the Olmecs, or whether they came up with their own language and writing system independently.

Either way, the Mayan writing system—commonly known as "Mayaglyphs"—was more developed, and made use of symbolic representations, phonetics, and a clear alphabet; which could all be used independently or merged together. This resulted in an elaborate writing system, containing over 200 syllables and symbols.

Mayan writing is written in a block system. The alphabetical representations are structured into two vertical rows of blocks side-by-side. The script is read starting at the top left block, going horizontally, and then going to the row of blocks beneath it.

Some of the symbols used included basic outlines of animals, such as centipedes and fish, as well as skulls and faces.

The Mayans would have used natural resources for writing instruments, such as quill feathers and animal hair. Based on findings, different materials and thicknesses were used in order to create a variation of strokes based on the glyph desired.

It is highly probable, though not certain, that only a small percentage of the population were able to read and write in the Mayan script. This was seen as a sacred practice, therefore, it is likely that it would have been limited to the priests, as well as men and women of the upper class.

Recent decipherment of Mayan writing enables us to enter into the lives and feelings of the rulers and their people. The hieroglyphic stairway in Copan, Honduras, is one of the greatest tributes to Mayan literacy. This impressive structure contains over 1,200 glyphs, which tells us the entire history of Copan from its inception up until its end. This stairway is the longest single write inscription in Pre-Columbian America. Other works were books written on bark and folded into shapes resembling fans.

The Aztecs built off of what the Mayans had created, and with a little bit of adaptation, they also wrote and documented events in their daily lives, including religious writings.

Unfortunately, the conquistadors were not able to read the native script and deemed most of their works to be pagan, which led to the majority of it being burnt. In fact, the language was banned by the Spanish all the way up until the 18th century. Fortunately, there were a few written works that survived the destruction and could therefore help historians to decipher the knowledge of the Mesoamericans.

One of these works is now known as the "Dresden Codex" and contains the astrological findings of the native nations. Out of all that the Mesoamericans had achieved, this invention is what excites archeologists the most, as if they had not documented their progress, we would never know how they truly lived.

# Art

The art of the Aztecs still warrants tremendous fascination to this day. Through their art, they had an amazing talent of capturing their spirituality. It is unlike anything that we recognize from European civilizations.

Their cities were adorned with sculptures of all shapes, sizes, and subject matters. In sculptures of certain rulers, we can clearly identify a timeline of the person's rulership, as well as their character development. Some of the early sculptures will show a king that is still soft in features and young. The next will show him as being hardened and his facial features more matured and fierce. The grimace look is very common in people that were respected, or who were great warriors, as this attested to their bravery, fierceness, and god-like qualities.

Interestingly, when the conquistadors found some of the statues, they quickly reburied them, as they found the subject matter rather mysterious and frightening. The art had a way of capturing not only the physical features of a person, but it also told the tale of their psyche and spiritual identity. This was not something that the Spanish wanted their people to see, or their younger generations to be influenced by. This was a blessing in disguise as it allowed archaeologists to find these statues during excavations at a later time period.

The spectrum of what could be carved and shaped was very broad, ranging from large statues to small and intricate works of art. They also built complicated looms, which were used for weaving clothes. Their wardrobe was considered a form of art, as well as storytelling, as they often wore bright designs with a lot of symbolism.

# Buildings

The great pyramid in Tenochtitlan has two temples on the top of its large stairway. The south-facing temple is where the Aztecs would hold rituals honoring the war god during winter months, and the north-facing temple is where they would honor the rain god during summer months. The pyramid was constructed so precisely that the sun would rise directly between these two temples, creating an awe-striking sight.

The precision of their structures is largely credited to their knowledge of the cycles of nature and the cosmos. They were able to study the movements of the sun in order to align their buildings in such a way that it would create a daily performance of symbolism between nature and man-made temples, further strengthening the bond between man and god.

Although the Egyptians were the first to construct great pyramids, the Mesoamericans built far more in quantity, and the Americas are currently home to more pyramids than the rest of the world combined.

It is estimated that the first Mesoamerican pyramid was built in approximately 1,000 B.C.E, with its construction continuing up until the Spanish conquest. These early pyramids were primarily made of earth, and thereafter overlaid with stone. They were usually constructed with a step shape, which would allow access to the top of the flat-topped pyramids for rituals and other ceremonies.

Unlike the Egyptians who used pyramids predominantly as a means of burial or preservation, the Mesoamericans actively used their pyramids for religious purposes. They would even dedicate them to the gods, and would host trainings for younger healers and shamans within these structures.

Some of their cities were extremely big. For instance, the Aztec city of Tenochtitlan was home to over 400,000 people. To accommodate this large population, architects needed to sufficiently plan and design layouts that would be able to house the entire population, as well as accommodate them during ceremonies and other public events.

# Rubber

Rubber is one of the most remarkable inventions by the Mesoamerican civilizations. It is not clear how they created a combination that would result in the elastic material, and many archaeologists suspect that they stumbled upon it accidentally, but this still attests to the constant contact and experimentation that the Mesoamericans had with nature. The latex properties were taken from the Panama Rubber tree, which was then mixed together with liquid from the Morning Glory vine. The combination resulted in a toughened, less brittle latex material. These two plants often grew close to each other, and before the discovery was made, they were used separately during rituals and ceremonies.

It is estimated that the Mayans constructed rubber approximately 3,000 years before Goodyear, who is often credited with inventing the chemical process to create rubber. The Mayans used rubber predominantly for ball games, and there is not much evidence as to other uses of the material.

To go with the rubber bouncy balls, the Mesoamericans also invented ball courts for their games. As with most items in the Mesoamerican culture, the ball games were not just for pleasure. The courts were often placed at the foot of the religious temples and were especially dedicated to the gods. The most common game, called "Pok-A-Tok", was a combination of football and basketball. However, the ball could only be passed and shot through the elevated hoops by using the thigh or the hip. This was extremely intricate and taxing on the body!

The ball games could last up to 20 days at a time. There was no such thing as playing for fun in the Mesoamerican world. The victors would win the belongings of the losing team members, and the losers would risk being sacrificed. Needless to say, the stakes were high, and this was not a game that was taken lightly. More than 1,300 ball courts have been found in the Mesoamerican region during excavations.

The game could either be played as a sport, or it would be played out as a drama, including costumes and a plot. As this game had such significance to the people, the courts were usually situated at the center of the city with ample space for every individual to gather and watch the game unfold. Once archeologists discovered a pattern that courts were centralized, it made their job of determining each city's center easier, as they could then identify and map other important structures from that central point.

In addition to rubber's use for sports in Mesoamerica, it is also believed that they could have used different variations and levels of hardness of the rubber material to make some form of footwear, such as sandals.

# Mathematics

The concept of zero was invented by the Mesoamericans an estimated 100 years before its introduction to the Europeans by India.

Their mathematical numerals only consisted of three main symbols: 0, 1, and 5. They used these three symbols to note all of their numerals up to the number 19.

A large number of Mesoamerican dates and estimations are quite accurate, which shows the efficiency of their calculations and numeral processes.

The mathematical symbols were a mixture of shell-like illustrations, dots, and dashes. Furthermore, they wrote their dates and other calculations vertically—as opposed to the conventional modern way of writing horizontally—which made them able to complete sums and estimations quickly.

Some of their numbers were considered numbers of importance, such as the number five, as this is the amount of digits on a human's hands and feet. In addition, certain numeral values were assigned to gods.

# Chocolate

While the Mesoamericans certainly did not invent the cocoa bean, they discovered its potential and various ways in which it could be used.

Chocolate was first discovered and consumed as a beverage, hence the name, which derives from the Nahua word "xocolatl", translating to bitter water. There was no sugar in the Central American region up until the arrival of the conquistadors. The Mesoamericans would transfer the liquid from the cocoa bean from one gourd to another repeatedly, until it formed a frothy beverage which they would enjoy.

They soon began to experiment with chocolate and would prepare it in different ways, as well as combine it with various ingredients. Due to it not being sweetened, the Mesoamericans found that the taste paired well with spicy foods, such as pepper and chili, as well as being mixed into cornmeal.

As chocolate was such a delicacy among the people, they believed that it was a food from the gods. For this reason, it was mainly consumed during rituals, ceremonies, or celebrations such as marriages. Once the Mayans discovered that the beans were the most flavorful when dried, simmered, and ground, it then became a form of currency.

Aside from chocolate, another popular snack that the Aztecs had come to discover and popularize was popcorn. The Mesoamericans are known for having an intricate relationship with corn, and it was only a matter of time before they discovered the effects that heat would have on corn kernels. Strangely enough, the Aztecs did not consume the popcorn, but rather used it as a means to decorate and adorn their clothing items and headdresses. The conquistadors would later describe corn that resembles little white flowers that was worn by the elite.

# Illusions

The Mesoamericans enjoyed playing around with optical and auditory illusions. When they had discovered the movements of the planets, they were able to create optical illusions that make use of shadows and sun positionings.

The most famous example is the Temple of the Pyramid Kukulka in the Mayan city of Chichen Itza. When the sun reaches a certain peak during the equinox, there is a shadow that is cast over the temple's staircase, which connects to the sculpture of a snake's head and gives it a complete body that drapes on either side of the temple. Ultimately, this represents the feathered serpent god. The Mayans must have established the movement of the sun and precisely designed the temple with the goal of creating the shadow effect. This illusion alone draws more than 25,000 tourists from around the world each year!

The Mayans, and later the Toltecs, believed that the descent of the serpent during the equinox was a great spiritual breakthrough that allowed them to communicate with their god on a more personal level. The setting was dramatic and awe-inspiring for the population and heightened their spirituality, even if only for a few minutes during the year.

Auditory illusions were also popular in Mesoamerican cities. They would often make sounds echo, or play out a song in temples and caves. In the same temple of Kukulka, something astonishing would take place: The priest would stand facing the 91 step staircase and clap his hands together, causing a sound that resembled a chirp, followed by a snap, which would echo back to the audience. The chirp is said to mimic one of the birds native to the area, and the snap is a similar sound to that of the tail of a rattlesnake.

To this day, audio engineers have been inspired by this auditory illusion, and it is still a phenomenon that is studied and used in teaching practices. The fact that this illusion was created intentionally speaks volumes on the scientific understanding of the Mayan civilization, and once again leaves us in awe of their abilities, which were beyond other ancient civilizations. The illusion can still be heard today when visiting Chichen Itza, and when one imagines a highly spiritual population of the past going through the entire procession from the serpent god shadow to the magical sounds, it is easy to see why the Mayans would place their worship at the pinnacle of civilization.

In other temples, the Mayans would ensure that sound was easily projected, and that the population was able to easily hear any speeches, public addresses, or chants that were given from the temple. Engineers have found that some of these temples could amplify sound over 350 ft away, which is approximately the equivalent of a football field!

In caves, the Mesoamerican civilizations would sometimes also create audiological illusions in which either echoes, songs, or spirit-like sounds could be heard. Hearing such sounds would completely unnerve any visitor or explorer in the region, who would sometimes suspect dark magic was involved, especially considering that these were not usual techniques used at the time.

# Chapter 7:

# Astrology and Beliefs

In ancient American civilizations, there was no real distinction between religion and science. The two often went hand-in-hand, and most of the scientific work and research was performed by priests or religious men of the time.

Despite this, their scientific knowledge and abilities were advanced and accurate for the time. The ancient cities contained observatories and libraries, which were used for cosmic and religious research, and the documentation thereof. Some of these cities, such as the Mayan city of Copan, had been found to be so well-equipped scientifically that it could be compared to some of the great intellectual cities of the time, such as Alexandria and Athens.

The Dresden Codex, which is one of the few surviving written works of the Mayans, contains predictions of the solar eclipses and movements of the planets. Through this codex, we are able to see how advanced the astrological knowledge was, as well as the extent of their research.

## Cosmic Science

The Mesoamericans had a very elaborate cosmic system. During excavations of various cities, such as the Mayan city of Tikal, it was found that the layout of the city was based off of the Mesoamerican's interpretation of the cosmic order. As a nation that has constantly searched for an explanation of nature in the cosmos, they spent a lot of time studying the skies. They then turned the earthly cities into a mirror image of their interpretation of the heavenly.

For this reason, science and religion are very much linked in the understanding of the Mesoamerican civilizations. Their cities on Earth follow a pattern of the cosmic order and their ritual centers, and the practices therein, are what ensure that humankind maintains the order of the universe.

Even through the studying of the cosmos, the Mesoamericans would interpret the movement of the planets and the stars as gods that were traveling celestially between destinations. It is therefore evident that their interest in science was largely due to their devotion to the gods that they believed created and ruled the cosmos.

## Calendar

The religious calendar, called the "Tonalmatl", was split into 13 months altogether. Each month was dedicated to a different god, and the month that one was born in would determine which god the individual would pray to. Prayer would also be determined by serious life events. For example, if one fell ill, they would need to pray to the god that dominated that month.

Unlike other civilizations that viewed time as a continuation, the Mesoamericans believed it reset each day at sunrise. A god would be assigned to oversee that day and would essentially "clock out" at sunset. The next day was another god's responsibility. Therefore, a set ritual would need to be performed on a daily basis for the god of the day.

The Mesoamericans placed great importance on their calendar systems. Like we view the Zodiac today, they believed that the time, day, month, and year that you were born in would hold significance on the events for the rest of your life. Due to this reliance, the Mesoamericans had an extremely advanced knowledge of astrology for their time. They had become accustomed to picking up patterns in the cosmos and were able to tell when certain phenomena would take place, such as solar eclipses.

Another astonishing factor of the Mesoamerican astrology was that their calculations and observations were incredibly close to those of the modern world. For example, they calculated a calendar year to be 365.242 days, whereas our modern day calendar is set at 365.2425 days.

In addition, the modern day lunar month is 29.53059 days, while the Mayan calendar has 29.5308 days in a lunar month, which also demonstrates their accuracy.

## *Aztec Sunstone*

During repair work that was ongoing in Mexico City in the 1700s, a remarkable stone artwork piece was uncovered. At the time, archeologists could tell that it was a piece by the Aztecs, but what it was exactly and the story that it told was yet to be unveiled.

This was not a small artifact. Rather, it weighed over 54 pounds, was 39 inches thick, and was 141 inches in diameter with a circular shape.

The inscriptions were quite detailed, as this was one of the artifacts that the conquistadors had unearthed, but later decided to rebury due to the subject matter of the carvings.

At the center of the circle, the sun god is depicted at the time of his death, which is said to occur during an eclipse, as per the Aztecs' prophecy of the ending of the world. The god also had a knife in lieu of a tongue, which is another symbol of death.

The center was also surrounded by a calendar system, which highlighted the fourth day, Olin, which recurs every 260 days per calendar cycle, and is the date when the sacrifice of a human would need to take place. The Aztecs believed that on these specific days, the world would end, and therefore, blood would need to be shed in order for the sun god to keep the world in existence. The depiction of the god in the center of the stone is surrounded by hands holding human hearts, which is a testament to the sacrifice that is made to the god in order to prevent his death.

The outer circle of the stone is carved with fire serpents, which represent the sun in dry season, once again depicting an unhealthy environment with a higher risk of death.

Based on these findings, archeologists concluded that the stone was not merely a piece of artwork or a generic calendar, but rather, that it was a clear cut conception of time. More precisely, it was used to track the days when human sacrifices needed to be made.

The stone is thought to be a monolith taken from the Xitle Volcano, which was close to 14 miles away from the Aztec capital city of Technotichtlan. It would have taken numerous men to carry the stone that distance manually. Based on research and careful analysis, it is probable that the carving dated back to anywhere between 1502 and 1521. Some historians suspect that the stone was originally painted and adorned. However, due to the time that has passed, as well as the conditions beneath the ground in the burial period, the stone has lost any color that it could have once had.

Today, it is one of the most famous stones from any Mesoamerican empire, and its housed in the National Museum of Anthropology in Mexico City. There are also several replicas that can be found in other museums around the world.

# Religion

There is no shortage of gods in the Mesoamerican societies, as they served and worshiped approximately 250 different gods, each in control of different aspects of life. It was believed that some lived in the sky realm, while others lived in the underworld. The gods were honored regularly through music, festivals, banquets, dances, and sacrifices. If the gods were displeased, it could lead to famine, droughts, and natural disasters.

The majority of the Mesoamerican cultures set their religious beliefs at the center of their entire society, and saw its success or failure as correlated. In other words, they believed that the happiness of the gods affected everything, including agriculture, trading, and weather conditions. They believed that the gods could intervene in everyday life, so it was crucial that they were kept happy to avoid any bad fortune.

They believed that Earth was the last planet to be made in a series of creations. Earth occupied a position between 13 heavens and nine underworlds. Plays and performances often depicted the creation of Earth, as well as the individual stories of the gods. The performers would dress up and wear decorative masks, animal skins, and colorful feathers.

For the Aztecs, there were two principal gods: Huitzipochtli, the war and sun god, and Tlaloc, the rain god. Both had their own temples on top of Templo Mayor Pyramid. The sun played a major role in the Aztec belief system, which emphasized the importance of the appearance of the sun to their everyday lives, as well as to the items that were dedicated to this god.

The Mesoamerican civilizations would often carve life-like statues of the gods with different types of materials, including amethyst, crystal, gold, and silver. The statues were also adorned with colorful feathers.

The priesthood had its own class system altogether. There were elite and senior priests, as well as lower level priests who attended to minor matters. Priests were required to be celibate and sober. If a priest was found to have committed an offense, the consequences were severe.

The ideologies of the people became one of the biggest driving forces behind the building of the Mesoamerican civilizations. While most of Europe was in the Dark Ages, incredible cities were rising up in the Americas.

Even though the Europeans were able to conquer and change the South American cities to what they are known as today, the spirituality of the Mesoamerican nations has remained. Many of the existing descendent communities are still rooted in the spiritual rituals and traditions of their ancestors.

## Human Sacrifices

The rulers were often chief priests who would be in charge of performing sacrifices, rituals, as well as ensuring that the gods were pleased. Human blood was often dedicated to the gods, as this was seen as the most potent offering.

During trying times, or in seasons of drought, the Mesoamerican civilizations wouldn't hesitate to offer human sacrifices to appease the gods and turn the odds in their favor.

In some cases, as with the Mayans, human sacrifices were reserved for special occasions, such as the dedication of a new temple or the crowning of a new king. The Mayans also believed in a quality sacrifice, so offering a person of elite status was preferred.

The Aztecs, however, believed in sacrificing quantity over quality. They would often start wars, which would be known as "Flowery Wars", in an effort to capture many enemy prisoners with the sole purpose of performing sacrifices. Once the Aztec were satisfied that they had enough prisoners, the war would end. The most prestigious offerings were the warriors who had shown great bravery and strength during the battle.

In all three civilizations, the ritual calendar was extremely important, as it would determine when a sacrifice needed to happen, so an accurate track record was kept.

The sacrifices would take place in three main forms:

- removal of the heart and the victim being decapitated

- hand-to-hand combat against a group of elite warriors

- during a drama or performance, where the victim would play the role of either a god or an individual that needed to be killed

Being chosen for sacrifice was considered to be one of the greatest honors, and many faced it with a sense of pride and privilege. While blood-letting was open for members of all social classes to perform as a personal tribute to the gods, sacrifice was usually reserved only for the elite, and was considered the highest form of death.

The Aztecs believed that the sun would cease to rise if blood-letting or sacrifices were not performed. In certain Aztec ceremonies, thousands could have been sacrificed over a four-day period. The conquistadors, including Cortés and his men, had witnessed some of these ceremonies and it completely horrified them.

It was a strange contrast for a civilization that was so advanced and talented to also be devoted to a primal ritual like human sacrifice. But the Mesoamericans put their devotion to the gods above all else, including human life.

## Ceremonial Knives

Special ceremonial knives, called "Tecpatl", were carefully crafted and put together for warriors' use, as well as for sacrifices.

Many of the knives found are traced back to between 1400 B.C.E. and 1500 B.C.E., and some date even further back.

They were usually approximately 12 inches in length and 4 inches in height, which made them practical for carrying around and using in a swift manner.

The handles were carved with precision and detail, usually from cedarwood, and adorned with various precious stones, including turquoise. They were ordinarily shaped in the form of a warrior or an animal, such as the jaguar or ocelot. The blade was extremely sharp and made from obsidian.

During excavations, archeologists tested the blades and found traces of human muscle and skin, which confirmed their suspicion of the knives being used for religious ceremonies and sacrifices.

## Burial

The burial rituals and traditions among the Mesoamerican civilizations were unique and each death was honored in its own right.

They believed that there were a total of 13 heavenly realms and an underworld. If one died a tragic or heroic death, then they would automatically go to one of the heavens. However, dying an ordinary, peaceful, and natural death would lead to the underworld.

The social status and, in some cases, the occupation of an individual would determine what would happen to their bodies once they died. It was not uncommon for the Mesoamericans to place items in the graves of the deceased when burying them, as they believed that these items would travel with them into the afterlife. For example, they would be buried with all of their possessions, a gift for the god of the heavens or the underworld, as well as necessities for the journey, such as food and weapons.

The king was usually buried with a red dog, which was sacrificed for the purpose of accompanying and protecting the king in the afterlife. Nobles or wealthier families were buried with valuable items, such as jaguar hide and jewels. Infants were often buried with carved representations of a uterus to symbolize the return of the infant to the womb.

Before the burial or the preparations took place, a small figurine of the person was usually crafted, and family members would take turns singing praises to the figurine before it was burned. There was then a long period of mourning, which usually lasted approximately 80 days before the burial took place. During this period of deep mourning, widows were forbidden from washing their bodies, faces, hair, or clothes. After this, the community would come and scrap off the dirt from the widow's body and place it on a piece of paper to be laid in a designated place in the village made for this specific purpose. While this whole process may seem extremely odd, it was a way for the family to gain complete closure from the death, and was a physical representation of what was happening emotionally.

In preparation for the burial, the eyes of the deceased were shut and water was poured over their head as a symbol of cleansing, as well as a reminder of the fluidity of life and death. Typically, the garments that were worn had to symbolize the occupation or the duties of the deceased.

The Mesoamericans did not limit themselves only to burials, and the higher the social status of the deceased, the more likely a cremation would take place. The ashes would then be collected in beautifully adorned vases and buried under the house of the deceased, along with important items for the journey to the afterlife, such as food.

One of the most surprising factors of a Mesoamerican death and burial process was that the families would hire professional mourners to help them grieve the lost family member. The Mesoamericans embraced the ability to cry and would often have outbursts of emotions, which was completely normal to the entire community. Accounts from conquistadors would attest to how the Aztecs would cry out, sometimes even resembling howling, and find enjoyment in their state of desperation and sadness.

The professional mourners were hired for just that reason: They would cry out and wail with the families and at funerals, and encourage each family to do the same. They were ultimately in charge of creating a somber atmosphere and would be the choir leaders for the rest of the population to follow and join. Dancing was also a common activity alongside the crying and wailing. This was really the performance of a lifetime for the Europeans, who were completely stunned by these crying, dancing widows.

Once the body was buried, it would not remain untouched in the ground. The Mayans would often retrieve the bones after a few years and would later rebury them along with a new set of supplies for the afterlife. In the case of a high-profile person, the bones were dug up and painted red before being reburied.

The bodies were also often buried in different positions. The two most common were either lying down on the back or in a crouching position, which is also depicted often in Mesoamerican art and sculpture.

## Nature and Animals

The Mesoamericans held a special reverence and respect for natural places, elements, as well as animals. The gods often represented the elements, such as earth, rain, and sun, as well as consumable elements like maize. They saw the new growth of maize crops as a spiritual rebirth of the soul.

Due to living in a region that saw extreme climates, as well as volcanic activities and natural disasters such as earthquakes, the Mesoamericans saw the Earth as being a sacred and living being. In their book of creation, it tells the story of how humans came to end up on Earth, which is seen as a being that needs nurturing, worshiping, and care. Humans were the fortunate chosen beings to take on this responsibility of respecting Earth's divinity. Humans are therefore required to perform rituals which bond them to nature, and by extension, to the heavens. If this responsibility was neglected, the whole universe would cease to have meaning, and extreme catastrophes would take place on the Earth.

While animals were generally respected, only certain animals were significant to the civilizations and their beliefs. This significance was generally reserved for animals that were feared and powerful predators, such as the jaguar or the eagle.

The Mesoamericans believed that these animals were not mere beasts, but that they were powerful and supernatural beings that could transform themselves into fierce creatures. Many of the religious artworks found from the Mesoamericans showed creatures that were a mix of man and animal, such as the representation of the were-jaguar, which was a common theme.

The jaguars' pelts were often worn by priests for religious ceremonies, as well as by elite warriors for combat. The pelts could also be displayed in households, or used as rugs; however, these use cases were reserved for people of authority only.

Large sculptures of jaguar heads were discovered, which is where some of the sacrifice victims' hearts would be placed as offerings to the jaguar god.

The jaguar and the eagle were often depicted together as companions. This is due to the jaguar being the predator of the earth, and the eagle the predator of the sky.

These animals are still represented in South American culture to this day. From street art to names of soccer teams, the jaguar remains a prevalent cultural theme that originated from Mesoamerican depictions.

Today, the contemporary Nahua religion is heavily influenced by Catholicism, which was instilled upon the arrival of the Spanish conquistadors. However, the descendants of Mesoamerican civilizations have tried their best to preserve what they were able to from their ancestors.

## *Music*

Music is a common denominator that can be found in almost every single civilization, modern or ancient, throughout the entire world. While modern day music is predominantly for leisure and entertainment, the music in most ancient civilizations was used to worship and celebrate their gods.

The Mesoamerican civilizations were no exception to this, and music would often be performed during rituals and ceremonies linked to their religious traditions. Music played a significant role in Mesoamerican culture due to its importance within their religious belief systems. The Aztecs considered music so vital that it was even required to be taught to children as part of their core curriculum.

Various instruments have been discovered during excavations, all of which were made from different materials, which created unique sounds. The main instruments were as follows:

- drums - both large and small, which were made using wood, as well as animal hide, and in some cases turtle shells

- rattles or rattle sticks - made from clay and filled with beans

- rasps - used from various animal bones

- trumpets - made from shell (often conch or snail) or clay

- whistles - made using wood or clay

An instrument vaguely resembling a guitar was also found, which was created using a gourd. With these instruments alone, they had great orchestral abilities. They were able to synchronize each individual sound to create a symphony of notes and melodies, which would be accompanied by dancers and worshippers.

Although modern day musicians have tried to replicate what they would assume to be ancient Mesoamerican music, there is no concrete record as to the songs that they played. However, there are some Mayan and Aztec descendants who can recall the tunes and reproduce them. By experimenting with each instrument as it would have been built by the Mesoamericans, as well as playing them as a group, historians could get a close approximation of what the traditional music at the time would have sounded like.

Once again, Spanish accounts of Aztec culture have been a great help to historians in understanding the role that music played in their day-to-day operations. These accounts confirm that music was vital to everyday life and was cemented in the routines of the Aztecs. Not only was music performed at various rituals and ceremonies, but the Aztecs would often sing while going about their daily chores and responsibilities.

# Chapter 8:

# Unsolved Mysteries

Despite the amount of information that has been uncovered by archeologists, there are still a lot of questions and mysteries surrounding ancient civilizations. This is largely due to the fact that many of their writings have yet to be deciphered or have already been destroyed.

Many historians have wondered how a civilization that was able to erect complex pyramids never invented simple items such as the wheel, or made use of domesticated animals such as cows or horses, for their manual work and produce. The answer may not showcase a lack in their talents, but rather, may be due to their respectful relationship towards nature. Through studies of their beliefs, we see that they often saw animals as gods manifested in another form. Could this be the reason why they did not feel it right to put a cow to work, or milk it, for example? Or was this an idea that never occurred to them?

## Similarities

Another perplexing factor that remains a mystery for historians is the number of similarities between the Mesoamericans and other nations of its time, despite the fact that no communication was taking place between them. Even to this day, similarities can be found between descendants of the Mesoamericans that live in Guatemalan regions and the Asian cultures, especially in their relationship with nature and humanity.

## Pyramids

One of these elements is the construction of large structures and pyramids. Many have wondered how it came to be that the Mesoamericans, Mesopotamians, and Egyptians all came to have large pyramids that were accurately constructed without passing the idea onto each other. Several explanations have been theorized regarding the construction of pyramids, with the most popular being that their inspiration stems from a deeper desire in humans to bridge the gap between the earth and the heavens, similarly to the famous Tower of Babel.

Humans, especially those that believe in a supernatural or spiritual realm, tend to want to reach this realm, and therefore think that the higher they are physically, the closer they are to their gods. Could this be the ultimate reason for similar pyramid constructions that were done in close succession on totally different continents? It still remains a mystery that has yet to be solved.

## Beliefs

When studying the Mesoamerican religion, there are striking similarities with the ancient Asian civilizations. Both nations have a unique and special relationship with nature, which can especially be seen in the ancient Chinese dynasties. With the concept of Chi, both the Mesoamericans and the Chinese believed an energy exists in each individual that also affects other beings, circumstances, and nature.

There is also a likeness with the Egyptian belief system, in the sense that both cultures were polytheistic, having a dedicated god for every aspect of an individual's life and afterlife. They also both believed that gods could take on the form of animals, as we see with the jaguar in Mesoamerica and with the cat in ancient Egypt.

Even where nations are vastly separated by time and space, these examples demonstrate how the human mind can still create the same symbolism and meanings.

## Farming Techniques

There have been some similar farming techniques that have been found between the Mesoamericans and the Egyptians. Although the Mesoamericans had much harsher and more unpredictable natural conditions, which made their techniques more complex than others, there was a definitive likeness in their farming styles and irrigation systems.

# Treasures

One of the greatest mysteries is whether there is still a hidden treasure from the Aztec empire that is waiting to be discovered. When the Aztecs had a premonition that their empire would fall to the hands of Cortés, it is believed that King Montezuma II ordered their treasure, as well as many of their written works and discoveries, to be hidden in a secret place.

Many have attempted to find this hidden treasure, having traveled all across the Americas in search of it. Although there are accounts of many written Mesoamerican works being destroyed by the conquistadors, some have said that the Aztecs purposefully chose to hide their books together with their valuable gold in order to keep information about their civilization withheld from Cortés and his men. This could be another explanation for the lack of books that survived the Spanish conquest.

Conspiracy theories have emerged that clues about the hidden location can be found in the Mexican flag, as well as in other Aztec art. Many believe that it can be found in the city where the Aztecs originated from, Aztlan, and that this city could possibly now be underwater.

It is said that the treasure, if found, will be worth well over one billion USD, if not more, depending on what it contains.

# Astrology

The Mesoamericans' documented knowledge of science, mathematics, and astrology was one of the biggest astonishments to explorers who first came across these nations.

Although these discoveries stemmed from an immense amount of time, patience, and curiosity from the Mesoamericans, legends have emerged that they must have obtained this information from other sources.

One popular theory is that the cultures in fact stemmed from an existing nation already, such as the Egyptians or the Asians, and that they carried the information with them when traveling to the new land in Central America.

Alternatively, another theory postulates that the Mesoamericans received this information from supernatural beings who passed down their valuable knowledge of the cosmos.

The Mesoamericans knew a large extent about the planets, and were even able to predict equinoxes and eclipses. But juxtaposed with the sudden disappearance of some of their civilizations, it is to be expected that questions would arise as to how the Mesoamericans saw to these advancements.

# 2012 Mayan Calendar

One of the biggest mysteries of the Mesoamerican civilizations, which would go on to lead to panic, would be the abrupt ending of the Mayan calendar.

It is widespread knowledge that due to the ending of the calendar, many felt that the Mayans had predicted that the world would end on December 21, 2012. At the time, there were constant debates, discussions, and theories surrounding this prediction and how it would all play out.

The Mayans had a long count calendar, which spanned over a period of 5,125 years, from 3,114 B.C.E up until December 21, 2012. The calendar would come to an end on this date because it marked the conclusion of the 13th Cycle of Baktum. Historians and scientists alike understood that the Mayans saw this ending as a symbolic one, and that a rebirth would take place with a new calendar being created after the 13th Cycle of Baktum.

However, considering that the Mayans had already correctly predicted a few occasions, such as the Spanish conquest and the fall of the Aztec empire, many believed that the rebirth of the Earth was not merely in symbol form, but that the Earth would physically die and a new planet would be formed. As excavations were done, and more information was released on how the Mayans had an almost supernatural knowledge of the cosmos and were highly advanced, their credibility in the eyes of the general public went even beyond that of high-profile scientific organizations like NASA, who had completely rebuked the theories.

The ending of the world in 2012 was so highly discussed that Hollywood even jumped on the bandwagon in 2009 by releasing the movie, *2012*. This movie had the tagline, "We Were Warned", and in the plotline, an obvious destruction of the planet takes place, despite the information that the people had from the Mesoamerican calendar.

It didn't take long for theories to emerge on how the world would end. Many suspected a collision with another planet, natural disasters, or the appearance of a gigantic blackhole would be the cause of Earth's destruction.

According to a poll that was conducted by Reuters in the first half of 2012, approximately 10% of the worldwide population believed that the world would end, as per the Mayan calendar (Michaud, 2012). The poll was responded to by over 16,000 people all across the world. Results showed that the majority of the respondents who believed the Mayan calendar prediction were from the younger generation with lower income levels. Despite this, the poll demonstrates the impact that the Mayan's calendar had made on a global scale.

# Aliens

As with many civilizations that were incomprehensibly advanced for their time, it was only a matter of time before people started wondering whether the Mesoamericans were influenced by an otherworldly population with superior knowledge to Earth.

In 2011, a new documentary, titled *Revelations of the Maya 2012 & Beyond*, was in production and set to release the following year to coincide with the much anticipated end of the Mayan calendar.

News of this documentary quickly made the rounds, as it was set to expose and prove the existence of alien contact with the Mayan civilization. The President of Guatemala himself, Álvaro Colom, also discovered the documentary and requested that the government be directly involved in the production of the film.

Furthermore, the Mexican Minister of Tourism for Campeche also joined the production, and later confirmed to the media that there was proof of alien activity with the Mayans in the form of secret codices that were kept in underground vaults by the government for safety. The documentary was set to be specific to the Mayan city of Calakmul, where a supposed landing pad for spacecraft was found in the dense jungle, dating back approximately 3,000 years.

Although much attention was garnered, the production of the movie seemed to have lost momentum before its completion, and no further news was heard about the release of the documentary. The fact that the project came to such an abrupt halt spiked even more curiosity and suspicion on the matter from the public.

# Underwater Caves (Cenotes)

"Cenotes" are craters that have been naturally formed from limestone across the Central American peninsula, leading to amazing and breathtaking underwater caves. These caves have filled up with water, creating an underwater tunnel system, or even underwater lakes, due to their size.

Due to the natural circumstances of the region, and the constant erosion of rock formations, Mexico is home to over 6,000 cenotes, which is more than anywhere else in the entire world. Cenotes are of great benefit to the Mexican population, as they provide clean, safe, and drinkable water.

What makes cenotes so mysterious is not their formation, but rather, the extensive water that they contain. A large number of cenotes are found right in Maya territory, and up until recently, it wasn't clear whether the Mayans knew about these cenotes or had access to them. During recent explorations, however, divers found concrete evidence that the Mayans not only knew about this underwater world, but they interacted with it on a regular basis.

The Mayans often built their cities next to these cenotes, as it provided them with a source for freshwater. Similar to the Mayan cities, the cenotes can be found in random locations, including in remote areas that require passage through thick jungles to access, which has kept them well-hidden for thousands of years.

There are various types of entrances to these cenotes, most being through a steep hole in the ground, which can drop over 50 ft down before reaching the surface of the water! Even though the entry path may seem daunting, once inside, the caves usually contain large chambers which provide ample space for diving and swimming. However, it is imperative to have the correct equipment and an experienced guide for these excursions, as getting out of the cave is virtually impossible by one's own means.

Another type of cenote is one that is surface level and resembles a large lake. However, when entering the water, there is usually an intricate cave system below the surface.

For the Mayans, the cenotes were passageways to the underworld, which therefore provided direct access to the realm of the gods. It has been found that many offerings have been thrown into the cenotes in order to please the gods. These offerings were not simply limited to objects, but also included human sacrifices.

Archeologists and professional divers who have explored the cenotes used by the Mayans have noted how incredibly eerie and haunting it is to swim through caves containing hundreds of human bones dating back to over a thousand years ago, with most of which being impeccably preserved.

The mystery remains whether all these bones are from sacrifices, or whether the Mayans used the cenotes as burial grounds. However, due to the information studied on the Mayan burial methods, there hasn't appeared to be much information that would lead to believing that they practiced underwater burials, as often the deceased were buried under their houses and close to their families. The debate is still on-going, but if the cenotes were used for human sacrifices alone, this would demonstrate the sheer quantity of sacrifices that were performed in order for hundreds of bodies to be disposed of in one cenote alone.

Another mystery is that some of the skeletons can be found in a side-by-side position, which would have been difficult to achieve by simply throwing deceased bodies into the cenotes. This led archeologists to wonder whether Mayans had a means of getting into and out of the caves, or whether some people were thrown in while still alive. Only a handful of the 6,000 cenotes in Mexico have been explored, and there is still much mystery surrounding what could be found.

In the last decade, the largest underwater cave in the entire world was found in Mexico, now known as the San Actun cave. The cave, which is situated near Tulum, now covers a distance of over 200 miles, and traces of the Mayan civilization can be found throughout its interior. This discovery could lead to further information and insight into the Mayan civilization, and the role that cenotes played in their cultural and religious practices. Many also believe that, should any claims of hidden treasure be true, it would most likely be found in one of the thousands of cenotes that are well-hidden in the Mexican jungle.

# Chapter 9:

# Legacy

Despite the fact that the Aztec empire fell in the 1500s, and the Spanish conquistadors tried to erase what they had achieved, the ancient civilization's influence is still felt today. Over the hundreds of civilizations that are considered ancient, there are only a couple that can be recognized just by their name. The Aztecs and Mayan empires are certainly nations that fall under this category, and almost any individual will have at least a vague familiarity with these cultures.

The current Mexican flag in itself is a tribute to the Aztec nation, as this is the vision that is said to have appeared to them when looking for a new territory to settle in, and which ultimately led to the building of Tenochtitlan.

## Films and TV

In pop culture, there is a desire to educate the younger generations on the past of Mesoamerica. For this reason, a couple of popular animated movies regarding ancient civilizations have heavily referenced the Aztecs and Mayans. The first example is the movie, *The Road to El-Dorado*, which recounts the story of two Spaniards who find themselves on Cortés' ship heading to the Americas, where they search for hidden treasures and gold upon arrival. Through their adventure, DreamWorks gives the viewer a good depiction of Aztec life during the time, including the famous ball games.

Another animated movie is *Coco*, which tells the story of a young Mexican musician who accidentally finds himself on a quest in the Land of the Dead. This animation relays the message to remember those who have lived before us.

These movies have purposefully ensured that the viewer is left with a positive view of ancient Aztec and Mayan civilizations in order to ensure that their legacy is passed down to future generations, and that young viewers are inspired to look further into their Mesoamerican roots.

Apart from animations, certain elements from Mesoamerican practices have also been featured in action movies, such as in *James Bond: Spectre*, in which scenes from the Day of the Dead celebrations can be viewed.

Due to the eeriness of the Mayan sites, many other movies have been filmed there as well, especially in the action genre.

# Fashion and Art

Hints at Mesoamerica can still be found in fashion items, as well as in modern art, which pay tribute to these nations. The Mesoamericans wore colorful and patterned apparel, which made their outfits pleasing to the eye and allowed the wearer to tell a story.

In addition to clothing, Aztec fashion can also be found in jewelry design and body art. Typical trends in Aztec-inspired fashion include bright colors, bold and often triangular shapes, as well as prominent borders and sharp lines. As a direct nod to the ancient civilizations, typical Mesoamerican-inspired jewelry will feature jade and turquoise, or at least a resemblance thereof.

In terms of art, there are still a number of creatives who pride themselves on creating sculptures, ceramics, and portraits that are directly inspired by these Mesoamerican civilizations.

One such artist is Marcela Zacarias, who spent much of her childhood around Mesoamerican excavations sites in the Mexican region. Because of her experiences, she grew up with a desire to inform others of these civilizations with a creative touch that came naturally to her. Her works included paintings of codices and symbols, which she conceptualized at a young age. More recently, she has worked on sculptures that feature references taken directly from the ancient cities.

## Health and Beauty

Due to the Aztecs having a reputation of good health and a well-balanced diet, it is no surprise that many brands and companies have adopted an Aztec approach to their product concepts. For example, "The Aztec Secret" is a beauty product company that uses clay from the soil of the California territory as a means of healing the skin (Aztec Secret Health & Beauty, n.d.).

Diets and meal plans that follow the Aztecs' produce and consumption thereof have also become popular. The most common being "The Aztec Diet", which was put together by Dr. Bob Arnot (Aztec Diet: Chia for Weight Loss, 2013). Dr. Arnot encourages the partaker to cut out modern day food, and to instead focus on food items that were grown and eaten by the Aztec population. Common Aztec foods include chia seeds (which is the main focus of the diet), fish, quinoa, and beans.

## Tourism

It is no surprise that many cities and sites that were once home to the Mesoamerican nations are popular tourist destinations today.

Tour guides can allow visitors from all around the world to see the ruins that lie deep beneath the overgrown jungle, enabling them to place themselves in the shoes of ancient civilizations, even if just for a brief period of time.

Teotihuacan alone has over one million visitors each year, and there is a continued effort to educate both outside and native visitors on the great history of the nation.

There are quite a few locations containing ruins from the Mesoamerican civilizations which are open for tourism. No matter where you are in Mexico, there will be a ruin site close by to visit. However, some will require a bit more effort to find, depending on how deep into the jungle you need to go.

## Calakmul

This city, which is approximately 21 miles away from the border of Guatemala, is home to one of the tallest Mayan temples in Mexico. It is very remote, as it is situated in a dense jungle area, but it is one of the least crowded cities and well worth visiting. Tourists are permitted to climb the 150 ft tall pyramid and take in the incredible views from the top.

## Chichen Itza

As one of the greatest cities in Mayan history, Chichen Itza is the place where the Mayans experimented with complex illusions, which still remain a big attraction to this day!

The El Castillo pyramid is the main attraction, especially during the equinox. Other sites that can be seen here are the Sacred Cenote, the Temple of Jaguars, and the Tzompantli.

Due to its reputation, Chichen Itza can get very crowded and busy. This city is accessible from either Cancun or Valladolid.

## Coba

The Mayan city of Coba is home to one of the largest pyramids of the Mayan empire, the Nohoch. It is over 130 ft tall, but you will be allowed to climb to the top if you feel up to the challenge.

For the more laid-back visitor, a bike can be rented to ride around the territory, which is quite large with many different structures which can be seen throughout.

The journey to Coba can be made via bus either from Tulum or Valladolid.

## *Edzna*

This Mayan city is less well-known, however, it is home to one of the infamous ball courts that the Mesoamerican civilizations have become known for. There is also a pyramid and a palace which can be explored during the trip.

## *Ek Balam*

This smaller city is often excluded from the list of sites to visit, as it is much smaller and still under excavations. An advantage of visiting is that it tends to be one of the least crowded tourist sites. It is accessible via Valladolid. You will be able to see temples, palaces, and pyramids when traveling there.

## *Palenque*

This city, which was once a powerful Mayan kingdom, is situated in the heart of the jungle. Here, you may explore pyramids, temples, and palaces, as well as see various artworks. You may also explore the Temple of Inscriptions, which holds over 180 years of solid Mayan history, and the Temple of the Jaguar.

It is not a straightforward journey to get to this city, however, as it is in the remote part of the jungle. Once there, the setting is visually inspiring, as there is a nice play of light between the rays of sunlight and the dense trees.

## Templo Mayor

Home to the center of the Aztec empire, the Templo Mayor is a great place to start touring for Mesoamerican ruins. It is situated right in the center of Mexico City and surrounded by the great cathedral.

Unfortunately, due the takeover of the Spanish, it is primarily ruins, with little detail or information, so it can seem underwhelming. However, there is a museum which will allow you to gain insight into the lives of the Aztecs in order to fully understand what you are witnessing.

## Teotihuacan

As one of the most populated cities of the Mayan empire, with over 150,000 people at its peak, this is definitely a site that should be added to the list. It is less than an hour away from Mexico City, which makes it the perfect place for a daytime excursion if you are staying in the capital city.

A few notable things to see at Teotihuacan include:

- the Temple of the Sun

- the Temple of the Moon

- the Temple of Quetzalcoatl

In particular, the Temple of the Sun is the third largest Aztec pyramid in the world, so it is highly recommended to explore.

## Tulum

The city of Tulum is the only Mayan city which can be found along the coast. It has a unique fortress design, being perched on the cliffs overlooking the Caribbean sea. A high 2,500 ft wall surrounds the city on three sides. The most notable site at Tulum is the Temple of the Frescoes, however, the entire site in itself is mesmerizing to behold.

The city can be accessed from Cancun and is about a two hour drive. Alternatively, you may rent a bicycle and cycle along the coast to reach Tulum, all while viewing beautiful beaches and wild settings.

### Yaxchilan

Yaxchilan is a Mayan city that can be found along the banks of the Usumacinta River, which was skillfully used by the Mayans at the time to trade and commerce.

Due to this, it is only accessible via the river, which can seem daunting considering the wildlife that is in the surrounding areas, as well as the remoteness of the city.

However, the journey will be worth it, as you will be able to see unique temples and hieroglyphs.

# Day of the Dead

Dia de los Muertos, also known as the Day of the Dead, is a celebration that has been ongoing in Mexico for hundreds of years. It first gained popularity when the Spanish conquered the Mexican region and combined their celebration of "All Souls Day" with an ancient Aztec celebration dedicated to remembering ancestors. It is celebrated to this day, typically taking place on the first two days of November.

During this time, families set up altars in their households with candles, pictures of their deceased family members or ancestors, and any memorabilia that they may have held onto pertaining to that person. In some cases, the person's favorite food is also left out, as well as other traditional food and drink items that are consumed during the festivities.

Once the ceremony at the house is done, they will make their way to the graveyards to clean up and continue celebrations. The main idea of the Day of the Dead is that the wall between the dead in the spiritual realm and the living in the earthly realm is temporarily nonexistent. This allows direct contact and communication between the two, similar to a big family reunion that takes place once a year.

All around the city, skeletons and skull decorations are visible. In addition to respecting the dead, the Spanish population also embraces death as a natural part of life, much like the Aztecs did, who saw death as an honorable occurrence. In fact, the Aztecs were already using a collection of skulls as a means of honoring the dead at least a thousand years before the Day of the Dead was formally established in the 1500s.

# Farming

Recently, Aztec farming techniques that date back close to a thousand years have emerged in Mexico. With sustainable living on the rise, cities across Mexico have found value in looking to the past for ways in which their ancestors farmed, and have even reinstalled a canal and floating farm system for agricultural purposes.

Today, the canals are navigated using specially-designed flat bottomed rafts known as "trajineras". These colorful boats are used by farmers and merchants, and as guide boats for tourists.

Many of the canal systems, such as in the city of Xochimilco, date back to Aztec times. It is remarkable to see a watering farm system that once served the Aztec empire can still be used to supply food to the residents of Mexico today! By leveraging its canals, Xochimilco has become the world largest fresh produce market, which is now able to feed a large percentage of the population in Mexico City on its own.

This system is not only beneficial to the agricultural supply by serving as a sustainable means of farming, but it is also a significant reminder of the civilizations that previously occupied the Mexican territory, and a testament to the great engineering achievements of the Aztecs. To this day, one can find over 5,000 acres of chinampas in the region, however, only a small amount of the agricultural systems are still in use.

# Conclusion

Despite all that has been uncovered about the ancient Mesoamerican civilizations, there is still a lot that remains unknown, with many aspects lacking factual findings. It is unfortunate that much of the work and progress that the Mesoamericans had made has been lost. This loss is either due to natural circumstances, a lack of ability to adequately preserve delicate historical items, war and human destruction, or some combination therein.

The little that we do know about these civilizations, however, has only left us in awe and yearning to know more about the motives and achievements of the Mesoamerican natives. The amount of progress and knowledge that the Mesoamericans had was so advanced that it even took the Europeans, who were the most powerful nation at the time, by surprise. They not only wanted to settle into the land, but they also learned a great deal from their counterparts, and felt mysteriously unsettled by the superiority of the native population. While war between the conquistadors and the natives was likely, it is highly probable that their motivation behind wanting to completely destroy the ancient civilizations was backed up by a fear of this highly advanced population. This, coupled together with the evidence of intense religious practices such as human sacrifices, were mind baffling to Cortés and his men. As a result, they sought to end what they perceived as a threat, instead of trying to understand the Mesoamerican people at hand.

Perhaps this could serve as a lesson to humankind, namely, to allow each civilization to develop in their own way, and with their own advancements, in lieu of the most powerful nations trying to create a likeness between all civilizations across the globe. The consequence of the latter being that a large part of cultural history ends up lost. When each nation was left to their own devices, new concepts and theories that have never been explored before suddenly appeared, and each civilization was able to bring a new lesson to the rest of the world based on findings and reasonings within their own territories and circumstances.

It should be such an inspiration for us today to see a civilization that was very much underequipped and uneducated by modern standards make such a prolific name for their empires regardless, even introducing concepts to the rest of the world that had not yet been founded. Items that we take for granted today, such as rubber, mathematical concepts, and even the simple chocolate bar, have their origins in the Mesoamerican region. It is no surprise that many have resorted to explaining the significant advancement of the nation as being a result of contact with supernatural beings, as it is difficult to understand the origins of the Mesoamericans' knowledge and ingenuity.

Research into Mesoamerican societies is still being conducted, and with the development of newer technology and methods, archeologists are continuing to uncover many hidden gems and lost cities to this day.

As more is being uncovered, we continue to learn the extent to which ancient civilizations outperformed those believed to be leaders of the time in their unrivaled ingenuity. Many emerging nations can now safely claim the title of being "the first", whereas European nations were often given preference until recent times.

It is intriguing to consider what else the Mesoamericans could have achieved if given the chance to work alongside the Europeans, or if left to their own devices. In a short span of time, they were able to advance their society at a rapid pace. It is evident that the descendants of these nations still hold their ancestors close to their hearts, and in some ways, are seeking to continue the legacy and work that they had started.

However, hope remains that with new and increasing technological capacities, more information about the Mesoamericans will continue to emerge, and what we are seeking to achieve in future can be informed from what has already been discovered in the past. Considering even a simple topic, such as dieting, has led historians to look back into what these civilizations did, and how we can incorporate their lifestyle into our daily habits. If this is the case for simple matters, imagine how much more information can be learned about more complex topics, such as social structures and governing, from Mesoamerican civilizations!

Perhaps a lesson can be learned from the Mesoamericans and there is something deeper to be found within human beings that can link to civilizations and nations across the globe. The Mesoamerican civilizations, although completely isolated, were able to find similarities with nations that were across the oceans, such as in Asia or North Africa. These similarities still baffle the minds of many historians and are the subject of many debates. We can only wonder whether the Mesoamericans would have had the same sense of confusion had they known that, in Egypt, pyramids were also being built. Even though humans have found themselves spread across various locations and circumstances, there are traits that can be found in each nation that connect the human race together as a whole. By comparing the Mesoamerican civilizations against others, we see common desires that have been displayed since the beginning of time. A good example of this is the need to find a writing system and method of communication. This demonstrates the human desire to record their day-to-day activities and ensure that there is evidence of important life events. This is something that has continued in modern times, where individuals still track down life changing moments and seek to better improve their communication methods with others.

Another commonality that has been found across nations is the need to enforce a social structure or hierarchy system with certain laws and boundaries in place. This has, once again, been common practice since as far back as historians can go and is still found in every nation on the Earth today. Without needing to be taught, humans have recognized the necessity of having social structures in place in order to ensure harmonious and peaceful living in social groups. This is not only common in humans, but is also present across all of the animal kingdom; even down to the simple honeybees, whereby workers report back to a queen.

It is these primitive desires and instincts that drive humans to want to achieve more and develop their nations in order to fulfill the attributes that need to be manifested to ensure sustainable growth. The Mesoamericans were no exception to this, and much of what they achieved was backed up by a need to become a great and functioning empire. Unfortunately, their demise was unavoidable, and the extent of what they could have achieved will remain a mystery.

While we have only just scratched the surface into the lives of the Olmecs, the Mayans, and the Aztecs, we can only wait with anticipation for what has yet to be discovered. By continuing to uncover the mysteries of Mesoamerica, we seek not only to understand what occurred before us, but also to gain deeper insight into our own lives, desires, and habits, as well as broaden our insights into the nature of humankind.

# References

*About us – healing clay.* (n.d.). Aztec Secret Health & Beauty LTD. https://aztecsecret.com/about-us/

Adhikari, S. (2018, January 26). *Top 10 inventions of the Mayan civilization.* Ancient History Lists. https://www.ancienthistorylists.com/maya-history/top-10-inventions-of-mayan-civilization/

Alonso-Castro, A. J., Domínguez, F., Zapata-Morales, J. R., & Carranza-Álvarez, C. (2015). Plants used in the traditional medicine of Mesoamerica (Mexico and Central America) and the Caribbean for the treatment of obesity. *Journal of Ethnopharmacology, 175,* 335–345. https://doi.org/10.1016/j.jep.2015.09.029

Alvarez, L. [Lillian Alvarez]. (2021, May 5). *Medicine, herbs, ceremony in ancient Mesoamerica.* Youtube. https://www.youtube.com/watch?v=8BE461V6ys0&t=740s

Ancient Americas. (2020, May 30). *The Olmec legacy.* Youtube. https://www.youtube.com/watch?v=lSO-bFwMx2I

*Ancient Aztec clothing.* (2019). Aztec History. http://www.aztec-history.com/ancient-aztec-clothing.html

*Archaeological study of 24 ancient Mexican cities reveals that collective forms of governance, infrastructural investments, and collaboration all help societies last longer.* (2023, March 3). ScienceDaily. https://www.sciencedaily.com/releases/2023/03/2303031052 13.htm

*Archaeology and the Book of Mormon*. (2021, January 4). Saints Unscripted. https://saintsunscripted.com/faith-and-beliefs/the-restoration-of-christs-church/archaeology-and-the-book-of-mormon/

*Aztec and Maya law: Aztec social structure*. (2018, November 8). University of Texas Law. https://tarlton.law.utexas.edu/aztec-and-maya-law/aztec-social-structure

*Aztec art: A way of life*. (2018, June 14). History On The Net. https://www.historyonthenet.com/aztec-art-a-way-of-life

*Aztec civilization*. (2022, May 20). National Geographic. https://education.nationalgeographic.org/resource/aztec-civilization

*Aztec diet – get healthy slim body*. (2013, November 22). Healthy Celeb. https://healthyceleb.com/aztec-diet-get-healthy-slim-body/

Aztec diet: Chia for weight loss. (2013). Freedieting.com. https://www.freedieting.com/aztec-diet

*Aztec inventions*. (2019). Aztec History. http://www.aztec-history.com/aztec-inventions.html

*Aztec medicine*. (2020, January 13). Wikipedia. https://en.wikipedia.org/wiki/Aztec_medicine

*Aztec music*. (2018). Aztec History. http://www.aztec-history.com/aztec-music.html

Barnhart, D. E. (2020, September 3). *The Maya people still have so much to teach us*. Ancient Origins. https://www.ancient-origins.net/history/maya-people-0014207

*Basic Aztec facts: Aztec burials*. (n.d.). Mexicolore. https://www.mexicolore.co.uk/aztecs/kids/aztec-burials

BBC Reel. (2022, March 30). *The little-known "mother culture" that inspired the Maya - BBC reel.* YouTube. https://www.youtube.com/watch?v=vyGr4iakR64

Bhattacharjee, A. (2023, January 27). *Mesoamerican mythology of the cosmos and the creation of humanity.* Yoair Blog. https://www.yoair.com/blog/mesoamerican-mythology-of-the-cosmos-origin-of-humankind-and-the-maize/

Blakemore, E. (2022, September 7). *Who were the Maya? Decoding the ancient civilization's secrets.* History. https://www.nationalgeographic.com/history/article/who-were-the-maya

BlueWorldTV. (2016, February 5). *Mayan underworld | Jonathan Bird's blue world.* YouTube. https://www.youtube.com/watch?v=UyqFnr6K7b0

Brophy, M. (2022, July 23). *The ancient rubber people of Mesoamerica.* Ancient Origins. https://www.ancient-origins.net/artifacts-other-artifacts/rubber-people-0017050

Brumfiel, E. (2019). *Aztec women.* Mexicolore. https://www.mexicolore.co.uk/aztecs/home/aztec-women

Captivating History. (2020, September 8). *The Aztecs explained in 14 minutes.* YouTube. https://www.youtube.com/watch?v=urFpctOmJZY

Captivating History. (2020, June 2). The Maya civilization explained in 11 minutes. YouTube. https://www.youtube.com/watch?v=YW0rLAX3y-c

Cartwright, M. (2014, February 4). *Aztec ceremonial knife.* World History Encyclopedia. https://www.worldhistory.org/article/650/aztec-ceremonial-knife/

Cartwright, M. (2014, February 26). *Aztec civilization*. World History
    Encyclopedia.
    https://www.worldhistory.org/Aztec_Civilization/

Cartwright, M. (2015, November 23). *Aztec society*. World History
    Encyclopedia.
    https://www.worldhistory.org/article/845/aztec-society/

Cartwright, M. (2014, February 12). *Maya writing*. World History
    Encyclopedia.
    https://www.worldhistory.org/article/655/maya-writing/

Cartwright, M. (2018, April 4). *Olmec civilization*. World History
    Encyclopedia.
    https://www.worldhistory.org/Olmec_Civilization/

*Civilization.ca - Mystery of the Maya*. (n.d.). Canadian Museum of History.
    https://www.historymuseum.ca/cmc/exhibitions/civil/maya/
    mmp08eng.html

*Compare and contrast Egyptian and Mayans*. (n.d.). Internet Public Library.
    https://www.ipl.org/essay/Compare-And-Contrast-Egyptian-
    And-Mayans-FCAYUCJTZT

*Crises that destroyed civilizations practically overnight*. (2020, April 8). Grunge.
    https://www.grunge.com/200268/crises-that-destroyed-
    civilizations-practically-overnight/

*Cultural spotlight: Ancient Aztec funeral traditions*. (2018, February 9). Frazer
    Consultants.
    https://www.frazerconsultants.com/2018/02/cultural-
    spotlight-ancient-aztec-funeral-traditions/

*Cultural spotlight: Ancient Mayan funeral traditions*. (2018, February 2).
    Frazer                                    Consultants.
    https://www.frazerconsultants.com/2018/02/cultural-
    spotlight-ancient-mayan-funeral-traditions/

*Daily life in Mesoamerica.* (2016, May 21). Bridge Man Images. https://www.bridgemanimages.com/en-US/daily-life-in-mesoamerica/8113

*Day of the dead.* (2016, September 28). National Geographic Kids. https://kids.nationalgeographic.com/celebrations/article/day-of-the-dead

*Definition of cenote.* (n.d.). Merriam-Webster. https://www.merriam-webster.com/dictionary/cenote

Diaz, J. (2020, May 9). *How the Aztecs shaped the modern world.* The Foothill Dragon Press. https://foothilldragonpress.org/271076/intersections/how-the-aztecs-shaped-the-modern-world/

Discovery Documentary. (2016, October 7). *History channel documentary - History of America - Aztecs civilization.* Youtube. https://www.youtube.com/watch?v=gBjqU2fh3eI&list=WL&index=12

*Early Mesoamerican civilizations.* (n.d.). Students of History. https://www.studentsofhistory.com/early-mesoamerican-civilizations

Editors of Encyclopaedia Britannica. (2022, August 24). *Aztec. Encyclopedia Britannica.* https://www.britannica.com/topic/Aztec

EdYouToo. (2019, March 21). *Olmec and Maya civilizations.* Youtube. https://www.youtube.com/watch?v=uURRfJu4mNc&t=803s

*End of world in 2012? Maya "doomsday" calendar explained.* (2011, December 20). National Geographic. https://www.nationalgeographic.com/science/article/111220-end-of-world-2012-maya-calendar-explained-ancient-science

Epimetheus. (2018, January 5). *History of ancient Mexico, Mesoamerica Toltec, Maya, Aztec, Olmec, Zapotec history.* YouTube. https://www.youtube.com/watch?v=GY4tnSov_3E

Farquhar, M. (1996, July 10). *The ancient Olmecs. Washington Post.* https://www.washingtonpost.com/archive/1996/07/10/the-ancient-olmecs/4a27965b-0e64-4da0-bd34-01ccf33ecf93/

*Filming location matching "Chichén Itzá".* (n.d.). IMDb. https://www.imdb.com/search/title/?locations=Chich%C3%A9n%20Itz%C3%A1

Flores, A. P. (2020, October 16). *Meet the artist bringing Mayan and Aztec culture to a Seattle gallery.* Cross Cut. https://crosscut.com/culture/2020/10/meet-artist-bringing-mayan-and-aztec-culture-seattle-gallery

Gayatri, S. (2022, October 10). *The return of Aztec floating farms.* BBC. https://www.bbc.com/travel/article/20221009-the-return-of-aztec-floating-farms

*Gender roles in pre-Columbian Mesoamerica.* (2022, November 11). Wikipedia. https://en.wikipedia.org/wiki/Gender_roles_in_pre-Columbian_Mesoamerica

GHCHistory. (2018, July 2). Hist 1111 - *Mesoamerican civilizations.* YouTube. https://www.youtube.com/watch?v=wjKDaoMdOvY

Ghimire, S. (2021, June 4). *Top 10 ancient Mayan inventions.* History Ten. https://historyten.com/mayan-civilization/ancient-mayan-inventions/

Gunderman, R. (2019, February 23). How smallpox devastated the Aztecs – and helped Spain conquer an American civilization 500 years ago. PBS NewsHour.

https://www.pbs.org/newshour/science/how-smallpox-devastated-the-aztecs-and-helped-spain-conquer-an-american-civilization-500-years-ago

Hall, J. (n.d.). *Mesoamerica*. Catwalk Yourself. https://www.catwalkyourself.com/fashion-dictionary/mesoamerica/

*Health profiles: Aztec warrior v Spanish conquistador.* (n.d.). Mexicolore. https://www.mexicolore.co.uk/aztecs/health/health-profiles-aztec-warrior-v-spanish-conquistador

*Herbs & medicines | Mesoamerican cultures and their histories.* (n.d.). University of Oregon. https://blogs.uoregon.edu/mesoinstitute/about/curriculum-unit-development/stem/ethnobotany/herbs-medicines/

History.com Editors. (2020, September 9). *Aztecs*. History. https://www.history.com/topics/ancient-americas/aztecs

History.com Editors. (2009, October 14). *December 21, 2012*. History. https://www.history.com/topics/religion/december-21-2012

History.com Editors. (2009, November 9). *Hernán Cortés*. History. https://www.history.com/topics/exploration/Hernán-Cortés

History.com Editors. (2022, July 21). *Maya*. History. https://www.history.com/topics/ancient-americas/maya

History.com Editors. (2020, February 24). *Mayan scientific achievements*. History. https://www.history.com/topics/ancient-americas/mayan-scientific-achievements

History.com Editors. (2019, September 30). *Pyramids in Latin America*. History. https://www.history.com/topics/ancient-americas/pyramids-in-latin-america

*In Mexico City, the pandemic revived Aztec-era island farms.* (2022, June 30). National Geographic. https://www.nationalgeographic.com/magazine/article/in-mexico-city-the-pandemic-revived-aztec-era-island-farms

Innes, R. H. (2019). *Hernán Cortés. Encyclopedia Britannica.* https://www.britannica.com/biography/Hernán-Cortés

*Introduction to Aztec health.* (2019). Mexicolore. https://www.mexicolore.co.uk/aztecs/health/

*Jaguars/ocelots | Mesoamerican cultures and their histories.* (n.d.). University of Oregon. https://blogs.uoregon.edu/mesoinstitute/about/curriculum-unit-development/stem/ethnozoology/jaguarsocelots/

Kessler, S. (2021, May 20). *15 Mayan death rituals & ceremonies explained.* Join Cake. https://www.joincake.com/blog/mayan-death-rituals/

Khan Academy. (2018). *The Olmec.* Khan Academy. https://www.khanacademy.org/humanities/world-history/world-history-beginnings/ancient-americas/a/the-olmec-article

Lidz, F., & Dhaliwal, M. (2022, September 13). Unearthing a Maya civilization that "punched above its weight." *The New York Times.* https://www.nytimes.com/2022/09/13/science/archaeology-mayan-mexico.html

Magazine, S., & Recker, J. (n.d.). *Four Aztec burials found in Mexico.* Smithsonian Magazine. https://www.smithsonianmag.com/smart-news/child-burials-in-mexico-city-show-the-resiliency-of-survivors-of-the-end-of-the-aztec-empire-180980358/

Maya society. (n.d.). History's Histories. http://www.historyshistories.com/maya-society.html

*Mayan documentary to show "evidence" of alien contact in ancient Mexico.* (2011, September 29). The Guardian. https://www.theguardian.com/film/2011/sep/29/mayan-documentary-alien-mexico

McFadden, C. (2018, August 18). *9 incredible Mayan inventions and achievements and one they missed.* Interesting Engineering. https://interestingengineering.com/culture/9-incredible-mayan-inventions-and-achievements-and-one-they-surprisingly-missed

Merriam-Webster. (2022). *Merriam-Webster dictionary.* Merriam-Webster. https://www.merriam-webster.com/

Mesoamerican civilizations: The Olmecs to Cortés. (2012, June 11). Study.com. https://study.com/academy/lesson/mesoamerican-civilizations-the-olmecs-to-Cortés.html

*Mesoamerican herbals.* (n.d.). Dumbarton Oaks. https://www.doaks.org/resources/online-exhibits/epidemics/epidemics-english/mesoamerican-herbals

*Mesoamerica timeline.* (n.d.). World History. https://www.worldhistory.org/timeline/Mesoamerica/

Michaud, C. (2012, May 1). One in seven thinks end of world is coming: Poll. *Reuters.* https://www.reuters.com/article/us-mayancalendar-poll-idUSBRE8400XH20120501

*Music and materials.* (n.d.). Maya Archaeologist. https://www.mayaarchaeologist.co.uk/school-resources/maya-world/maya-music-and-materials/

Nalewicki, J. (2017, May 16). *From whispering galleries to echo chambers, these five architectural structures have extraordinary acoustics.* Smithsonian Magazine. https://www.smithsonianmag.com/travel/worlds-weirdest-echoes-where-hear-them-180963307/

National Geographic. (2018, April 29). *Ancient Maya 101 | National Geographic.* YouTube. https://www.youtube.com/watch?v=Q6eBJjdca14

*9 unsolved mysteries of the ancient Mayan civilization.* (2017, April 18). ViralTalks : Stories & Videos. https://viraltalks.com/unsolved-mysteries-of-the-ancient-mayan-civilization/p/

Nuckols-Wilde, C. (2019, July 28). *Teotihuacan's legacy.* Mesoamerican Studies Online. https://mesoamericanstudiesonline.com/2019/07/28/teotihuacans-legacy/

Nutty History. (2021, May 31). *What medicine was like in the Mayan empire.* Youtube. https://www.youtube.com/watch?v=qWYI82fEZl0

*Olmec civilization.* (2022, May 20). National Geographic. https://education.nationalgeographic.org/resource/olmec-civilization

Our History. (2021, September 7). *Exploring the incredible origins of Central America (Mayan/Aztec documentary) | Our history.* Youtube. https://www.youtube.com/watch?v=CRhTdFBhL6o&t=2324s

Paul & Mark. (2022, September 14). *10 important Aztec & Mayan ruins in Mexico.* Anywhere We Roam. https://anywhereweroam.com/ancient-ruins-mexico/

Peña, J. C. (1999). Pre-Columbian medicine and the kidney. *American Journal of Nephrology, 19*(2), 148–154. https://doi.org/10.1159/000013441

Phillips, M. (2019, July 23). *Architecturally sound: Part 3 - chirped echoes & colouration*. Supawood. https://www.supawood.com.au/news/architecturally-sound-part-3-chirped-echoes-colouration

Reuters. (2018, January 17). World's longest underwater cave system discovered in Mexico by divers. *The Guardian*. https://www.theguardian.com/world/2018/jan/17/worlds-longest-underwater-cave-system-discovered-mexico-divers-gran-acuifero-maya

Román, I. (2020, October 29). *Day of the dead: How ancient traditions grew into a global holiday*. History. https://www.history.com/news/day-dead-dia-de-muertos-origins

Scofield, B. *(2006). The twenty day-signs of Mesoamerican astrology.* Astrolabe. https://alabe.com/text/Scofield-20DaySigns.htm

Sergio. (n.d.). *The descent of the serpent in the Chichen Itza equinox*. Maya Peninsula. https://mayanpeninsula.com/chichen-itza-equinox/

*Sort by popularity - most popular movies and tv shows tagged with keyword "mesoamerica."* (n.d.). IMDb. https://www.imdb.com/search/keyword/?keywords=mesoamerica

Strauss, V. (2012, December 19). NASA's lesson on the end of the world. *Washington Post*. https://www.washingtonpost.com/news/answer-sheet/wp/2012/12/19/nasas-lesson-on-the-end-of-the-world/

Telesco, S. (2018, July 23). *Learning the Mesoamerican zodiac*. Astrology News Service. https://astrologynewsservice.com/articles/learning-the-mesoamerican-zodiac/

Than, K. (2010, December 18). *Ancient Maya temples were giant loudspeakers?* National Geographic. https://www.nationalgeographic.com/history/article/101216-maya-acoustics-speakers-audio-sound-archaeology-science

*The Aztec art of mourning.* (n.d.). Mexicolore. https://www.mexicolore.co.uk/aztecs/home/the-aztec-art-of-mourning

*The collapse of the Olmec civilization.* (2021, July 20). History in Charts. https://historyincharts.com/the-collapse-of-the-olmec-civilization/

The Editors of Encyclopedia Britannica. (2016). Maya. *Encyclopedia Britannica.* https://www.britannica.com/topic/Maya-people

The Editors of Encyclopedia Britannica. (2015). Mesoamerican civilization. *Encyclopedia Britannica.* https://www.britannica.com/topic/Mesoamerican-civilization

*The history and culture of Olmec civilization.* (2021, June 12). YouTube. https://www.youtube.com/watch?v=unayHy60ZnM

*The history of swimming: From the Maya to the Aztecs...and more.* (2022, August 9). Swimming World News. https://www.swimmingworldmagazine.com/news/the-history-of-swimming-from-the-maya-to-the-aztecs-and-more/

*The mystery of the lost ancient culture of the Maya.* (2014, June 4). Ancient Origins. https://www.ancient-origins.net/opinion/mystery-lost-ancient-culture-maya-001719

*The Olmec: Civilization & culture.* (2013, February 22). Study.com. https://study.com/academy/lesson/the-olmec-civilization-culture-quiz.html

*The search for Aztec treasure.* (2021, June 9). Treasures in America. https://treasuresinamerica.com/aztec-history/the-search-for-aztec-treasure-aztlan-montezumas/

*The secrets and significance of gold in Mesoamerica.* (2019, April 14). Glint. https://glintpay.com/en_us/blog/secrets-significance-gold-mesoamerica-2/

Tiesler, V. (n.d.). *Cranial surgery in ancient Mesoamerica.* https://www.mesoweb.com/features/tiesler/Cranial.pdf

Timeline - World History Documentaries. (2019, November 14). *Breaking the ancient Maya code | Archeology | Timeline.* YouTube. https://www.youtube.com/watch?v=RWH2CrSvm2g

Timeline - World History Documentaries. (2017, March 3). *Uncovering the lost Mayan city of La Corona | Quest for the lost city | Timeline.* YouTube. https://www.youtube.com/watch?v=5Nhsp26bN8U

Tomzak, M. (n.d.). Science, civilization and society. *Physocean.* http://www.physocean.icm.csic.es/science+society/lecture18.html

Townsend, C. (2019, November 1). *We learned about the Aztecs from their conquerors—but new research is letting them speak for themselves. Time.* https://time.com/5715476/aztec-history-myths/

*12 Mayan ruins in Mexico you must know.* (2022, August 4). Chichen Itza. https://www.chichenitza.com/blog/12-mayan-ruins-in-mexico-you-must-know

Vacations, I. (2022, November 2). *Exploring the history and traditions of Mexico's day of the dead.* Insight Vacations. https://www.insightvacations.com/blog/mexicos-day-of-the-dead/

Van Stone, M. [Mark Van Stone]. (2010, September 5). *Dr. Mark Van Stone - How Maya hieroglyphs are written - Demonstration.* Youtube. https://www.youtube.com/watch?v=630e2bFLbfY

Waugh, R. (2012, May 3). *Heads did roll: The blood and hair that proves Mexicans used stone knives for human sacrifice 1,000 years before Aztecs.* Mail Online. https://www.dailymail.co.uk/sciencetech/article-2138946/The-2000-year-old-bloody-knife-PROVES-ancient-Mexicans-practiced-human-sacrifice.html

*What did Aztec music sound like?* (2021, December 18). Sounds and Colours. https://soundsandcolours.com/subjects/travel/what-did-aztec-music-sound-like-63875/

*What were the surgery practices among the Aztecs?.* (n.d.). Mexicolore. https://www.mexicolore.co.uk/aztecs/ask-us/what-type-of-surgery-did-the-aztecs-practice

Wright, M. A. (2013). The cultural tapestry of Mesoamerica. *Journal of Book of Mormon Studies, 22*(2). https://scholarsarchive.byu.edu/cgi/viewcontent.cgi?article=1519&context=jbms

Made in United States
North Haven, CT
16 June 2023

37865233R00070